The Rubáiyát of Rumi

The Ergin Translations
Volume 4 of 4

The Rubáiyát of Rumi

The Ergin Translations
Volume 4 of 4

The Quatrains
from the
Osman-al Mavlavi Compilation
of
The Dîvân-i Kebîr of Mevlânâ Celâleddîn Rumi

Quatrains Compiled and Edited by
Millicent Alexander with Shahzad Mazhar

Introduction and Appendices by
Millicent Alexander

Powerhouse Publishing
Los Angeles, California
USA
www.ReadingRumi.com

Copyright © 2024 by Millicent Alexander

First published by Powerhouse Publishing 2024

All right reserved. No part of this book may be reproduced or utilized in any form or by any means, electronic or mechanical, including photocopying, recording, or by any information storage and retrieval system, without permission in writing from the publisher.

Thank you for respecting the author's rights.

Printed in the United States of America.
ISBN: 978-1-947666-15-3 (hardcover)
ISBN: 978-1-947666-16-0 (paperback)
ISBN: 978-1-947666-17-7 (e-book)
Library of Congress Control Number: 2022938928

Available from Amazon.com and other retail outlets.
Printed, bound and distributed worldwide by IngramSpark.

Book design and layout by Oscar Díaz Del Valle and Toni Norcross.

Typeset in Schoolbook,
with Duc de Berry and Study as display type.

The cover artwork and the artwork on pages 1, 11 & 249 are photographs of the original artwork created by Abu Bekir al Mavlavi for the Osman-Al Mavlavi Compilation of the *Dîvân-i Kebîr* compiled in 1367-1368 CE and registered as #68 and #69 in the Mevlânâ Museum in Konya, Turkey. These photographs, as well as microfiche of the entire al Mavlavi compilation, were commissioned by Nevit O. Ergin with permission from the Turkish Ministry of Culture and the Mevlânâ Museum in Konya, Turkey.

Calligraphy and illustrations of the musical instruments, Kaaba and Whirling Dervish are by Smaro Gregoriadou.

In Memory
of
Hasan Lutfi Shushud

Gratitude

Ergin was a spiritual giant. We are eternally grateful for his making such a remarkable contribution to the English-speaking world. We are also eternally grateful for the opportunity he gave us to immerse ourselves for the past seven years in these rubais.

We wish to express our gratitude, too, to Kavi Alexander, Yamil Alis, Zaid Alowayed, Kavous Barghi, Merâl Ekmekçioğlu, Banu, Evren and Zanep Ergin, Emre and Cengiz Ergin, Professor Mahmoud Ganadan, Jill Gluck, Edmond Gorginian, Jeferson Martinez, Toni Norcross, Haydar Pekdemir, Amy and Amit Singh, and especially: Oscar Díaz del Valle, John Morris, Dimitris Economidis and Smaro Gregoriadou.

Contents

Introduction 1
    Foreword 3
    Mevlânâ Celâleddîn Rumi 7

The Rubáiyát 11

Appendices 249
    Notes on these Translations 251
    The Importance of Islam in Rumi's Life 261
    Islamic and Sufi Terms Commonly Used in Rumi's Poetry 263
    The Role of Music in Rumi's Life 265
    Musical Instruments Commonly Referred to in Rumi's Poetry. 267
    The Story of Joseph and Jacob 270
    The Concordance 272
    Bibliography: *Mevlânâ Rubâîler* 288
    Bibliography: *The Rubáiyát of Rumi, The Ergin Translations*..289

Every shape in this old world is old.

Love is beautiful, fresh.

The one who looks for it is even more tender.

-*Divan-i Kebir,* Volume 10
ghazal 41, verse 467

Introduction

The most common theme in all of Rumi's poetry is Love, the kind of Love which can only be reached through total annihilation of the self. There are many, many quatrains which focus on this kind of Love, and they deserve the most careful of readings.

-Nevit O. Ergin

Foreword

Rumi is considered one of the greatest Love poets of all time. It is true that many of his poems describe his love for another human being:

> O beloved,
>
> if you want to know what shape I'm in,
>
> ask your eyebrows.
>
> Ask your curly hair
>
> about the state of my confusion.
>
> Ask your small mouth
>
> about the state of my heart.
>
> Ask your bewitching eyes
>
> about the state of my insanity.
>
> -Rubai 539 (Volume 2)

But to limit our understanding of Rumi's poetry to human love would be a colossal mistake. As he says:

> O Love, You are a boundless ocean.
>
> The desire which men and women
>
> feel for each other
>
> is just a drop of that ocean.
>
> -*Dîvân-i Kebîr*, Volume 11
> ghazal 76, verse 968

We all go chasing after or at least wish for earthly love. We love our significant other, we love our children, we love God, we love our job, we love to eat, we love sports and so on. That kind of love is symbolic love, practice love if you will. No matter how strongly we believe we love someone or something, that kind of love is minuscule compared to the Eternal Love Rumi talks about:

> Love is an ocean
>
> which has no bottom, no boundary.
>
> It is an ocean suspended.
>
> Love is the secret of the One
>
> who has no beginning of the beginning.
>
> All souls are drowned in Love. They live there.
>
> Hope is one drop of that ocean.
>
> The rest of it is fear of separation.
>
> -Rubai 1727 (Volume 4)

Rumi's poetry shares with us his spiritual journey to Love as he takes each step forwards and backwards. He starts out as a human and ends up as Nothing, having completely annihilated his self, dying before his physical death:

> Love is like treasure buried in the ground,
>
> hidden from the pious as well as the blasphemous.
>
> In order to get this treasure,
>
> I did what was needed.
>
> I undressed from my self,
>
> becoming completely naked.
>
> -Rubai 868 (Volume 2)

As Rumi states, he reached Love because he annihilated his self. Many Westerners confuse the world "self" with the ego. The ego is only a part of the self. The self is meant here to reflect all of one's being and becoming, one's doing, one's everything:

> Before you are cooked in the flames of your heart,
>
> you are nothing but wet kindling.

> Unless you tear up the body's cloak,
> the flames of Love cannot be your mentor.
>> -Rubai 1119 (Volume 3)

And Rumi tells us how fasting can aid us in the journey of self annihilation:

> Accept fasting as a beggar's basket in hand.
> Don't let it go.
> Let fasting be a way
> for you to beg on the way of God,
> so that God will award you with the Water of Life
> and your thirst will be satisfied.
> Fasting resembles a fragile jar. Don't break it!
>> -Rubai 1616 (Volume 4)

A second aid is the suffering which results from the submission to Love:

> Your Love grabbed me roughly by my shirt collar
> and put my wayward feet
> on a straight path towards my Beloved.
> Love said, "I am going to drag you over stones
> for a long, long time."
> I replied, "Keep on dragging me
> until I am completely matured."
>> -Rubai 701 (Volume 2)

Another point of confusion for many Western readers is Rumi's constant mention of the Beloved. Yes, as already mentioned, in some of the quatrains, the beloved is indeed a human being. But, once Rumi reached a certain stage in his journey, once his self had been annihilated, there was room for the Beloved to come out from behind the curtain.

> You have two hands, two feet, two eyes.
> That is true.
> But, it would be a mistake
> to count the heart and the Beloved as two.
> Saying "Beloved" is only a pretext.
> In fact, God is the Beloved.
> Whoever says God is two is an impious infidel.
> -Rubai 149 (Volume 1)

We are blessed to have had Rumi leave us all of these quatrains. Whether a particular one is an expression of Rumi when he was just starting out on his journey or one expressing what it was like after he reached Eternal Love, all of his quatrains give us a window into the experiences through which he progressed.

Have or will other humans reach the heights of Rumi? Regardless, we all can gain hope as we each strive on our own paths and allow Rumi's poetry to inspire us:

> I have been dissolved in the sea of purity like salt.
> There is no belief, no heresy left in me.
> Neither certainty nor doubt remains.
> A shining star has appeared in my heart.
> Even the seven levels of the sky
> have disappeared into that star.
> -Rubai 606 (Volume 2)

The Ergin Translations - 7

Mevlânâ Celâleddîn Rumi

Image Credit: The Granger Collection, Ltd.,
Historical Picture Archive/NY.

Mevlânâ Celâleddîn Rumi

According to Rumi's first biographer, Ahmet Eflâkî in his Arîflerîn Menkibelerî (written between 1318 and 1353):

> Mevlânâ...died on Sunday, December 17, 1273 at sunset. ...The next morning at sunrise, they took his coffin from the medresse and set off. Christians and Jews, Arabs and Turks, people from all religions and nations, pious scholars and rulers were present at his funeral. All went in front of the funeral holding their own holy books as entailed by their traditions. They were crying and reciting verses from the book of Psalms, the Old and New Testaments.
>
> They said, 'We understood the truth of Moses, Christ and other prophets from his clear statements; and we saw in him the nature and behavior of the prophets we have read about in our books. Just as you Muslims regard him as the Muhammed of his time, we also acknowledge him as the Moses and Christ of his time. We are his servants and disciples just as you are and we are even a thousand times more obedient to him.
>
> Mevlânâ is the sun of the truths shining over humanity and scattering the light of grace upon them. The whole world loves the sun. All houses are enlightened by his light.[1]

---

[1] Erdoğan Erol, *Mevlânâ's Life, Works and the Mevlânâ Museum* (Konya: Altunari Ofset Ltd. Şti, 2005),21.

Mevlânâ summarized his life with the words, "I was raw, cooked and burned."

He willed his friends not to lament after him. He believed that the day of death was also the day of rebirth and referred to it as Şeb-i Arûs [wedding day].

As for remembering him, he had written:

> Do not look for my grave in the ground
> when I am dead!
> My grave will be in the hearts of the learned.[2]
>
> -Hz. Mevlânâ

---

[2]Erol, *Mevlânâ's Life*, 23.

The Soul of the Universe never tires of lovers,
nor do lovers ever tire of Him.

-Rubai 1671 (Volume 4)

The Rubáiyát

There is nothing remaining in my ears
except the murmur of Love.

-Rubai 1776 (Volume 4)

We are the guests of the Moon and Jupiter tonight. 1399
We are all in love with the Beloved's face.
While drinking the wine of the Sultan of sultans,
we have attained every one of our wishes tonight.

My belligerent Beauty 1400
who has made wine-drinking His way
came tonight and sat in front of me like a bale of sugar.
He picked up His saz and started singing this tune:
"I am free of my self. I am happy now,
O, so very happy!"

1401 The wine which is forbidden to the body
is served freely to the soul of the one
who is free from attachments to this world.
Pour us more, O cupbearer.
Never say, "This is the end."
Who knows where our beginning is?
Or, our end?

1402 The time has come for Me to embrace you,
so I am turning your soul into a house of fire.
You are a gold mine hidden within the soul,
and I am throwing you into the fire
to burn out all of your impurities.

I danced in front of my charming Beloved, 1403
clapping my hands like a foolish drunk.
Because of His kindness, He watched me happily.
But, I don't know. How could I do such things?

I keep running with the hope of finding the Beloved, 1404
because my life has almost come to its end,
and I am still dreaming.
Assuming I will eventually find the Beloved,
how can I find the time which has already passed?

1405   The wine which is forbidden to the people
is served freely to the soul
of the wandering ascetic.
Beware, O cupbearer. Never say, "This is the end."
Who knows where our beginning is?
Or, our end?

1406   When this sorrow catches someone alone,
it takes the dress of humanity from his head.
He becomes such a strange soul
that he doesn't want anything and no one wants him.
How could someone become his friend
without knowing this sorrow?

In my search for the Beloved, 1407
my eyes cry like a river.
In seeking Him, I flow like water in a river.
That Beloved came to me at early dawn and said,
"Get up. It's time for Sema,"
not even allowing me a chance to make ablutions.

I am a grape, crushed under trampling feet. 1408
I turn wherever Love pulls me.
You ask, "Why are you turning around me?"
I am not turning around you.
I always turn around Me.

1409 I hear the sound of joy, the trumpet of that final day.

That sound brings me back to life, raising me to the sky.

The One who knows everything comes

to me suddenly,

bringing me so much beautiful news.

Yet, no one is aware of it.

1410 I learned this turning from my soul.

I turned around like this before I entered my body,

while I was pure soul.

They said, "Stillness and patience are better."

I said, "I will give you both of those for free."

My friend, I am prey, but I have also caught prey. 1411
I am idle, but busy at the same time.
And, my job is a very good and wondrous one.
You asked, "Are you planning to cut off my head?"
I said, "Well, my beauty,
I have had that notion in my mind."

O Beloved, because of Your Love, 1412
I am vanishing like the Moon.
You haven't been my guest for even one night.
Yet, You tell me to know this well:
"I am yours. I give you life. I am your soul."

1413   O sound of the rebab,

        I have caught a spark from you.

        There is One who plays the rebab in my heart.

        O Beloved, please don't pass through.

        Come in and be my guest.

        I have a place in my ruined heart for You.

1414   O my peace and happiness, since I have seen Your face,

        I have been saved from such terrible events!

        If I have broken any glasses at any of Your gatherings,

        I will send hundreds of gold-covered glasses to You.

Thanks to the wings of Your Love,   1415
the place of my heart is not in this house.
Your torment has become halva for my heart.
Although I have no complaint about Your sorrow,
wouldn't it be nice if You could hear my moans?

I tell my troubles to you with my stories.   1416
If you close your ears, I whisper them to you secretly.
I have come to the conclusion
that my sorrows please you.
You enjoy hearing all about them.
That is why I tell all of my sorrows to you.

1417 He is such a magic garden

that I have blossomed with His spring.

Once I bloomed, that garden answered all of my wishes.

When He made me drunk with His glass of glory,

I put my drunken head down and slept.

1418 When Love's unruliness

kicks out all of my thoughts,

by God, I become stronger and lighter.

If I go to the gallows one day like Mansur,[1]

I will receive messages from Him every moment.

---

[1] Hallaj Mansur, a famous Sufi martyred for his beliefs (858-922 CE).

He has come back! He has come back! 1419
I am opening the road for Him.
He is looking for a heart to seize,
and I am offering my heart to Him.
I yell, "Kill me. I am Your prey!"
He answers with a smile,
"Yes. I have you in My sights."

I was an ever-blooming rose garden thanks to You. 1420
After seeing You, my eyes became bright and shining.
I used to say,
"May evil eyes stay away from Your face."
But, might I be the one with the evil eye
which I have turned on You?

1421   My drunken heart had long been devoted to the tavern.

At that tavern,

I bought a glass of divine wine with my soul.

When my heart and soul fell in love with divine wine,

I gave both of them to the tavern as a gift.

Now, all my grief has disappeared.

1422   He walks gracefully over land and deep oceans,

leaving His lovers to sigh sorrowfully

in longing for Him.

You are not the only one who loves Him.

Everyone who sees Him falls in love with Him.

Because of the treasure He gave us in eternity, 1423
we have become His ruins.
Because of His story,
we have become one of His stories.
Alas, because of His covenant,
no one can separate his own home from His.

I have died from shame, 1424
because I have had to live without You.
I have taken leave of my soul,
because I have had to sit without You.
You willed our separation,
so I have had to exist without You.
I shed bloody tears because I am separated from You.

1425   I listen to the melodies of Your sorrow in my soul.
In fact, aren't all souls just tiny bits of Your sorrow?
They keep turning and shining
by the light of Your sorrow,
in the air of their longing for You.

1426   There is someone who constantly pains me.
My face is pale, my heart broken because of him.
Out of playfulness today, he hit me with his shoulder.
Thank God! I received a shoulder hit from him!

He is such a Sultan that reason has become His fool.   1427
He and my heart stay in the same house.
He sent a moth, saying, "I am yours,"
and hundreds of candles became moths to His light.

Some will be jealous of your dress   1428
or your lips which tell of your desires.
Others will be jealous of your bright face
or your wise and learned countenance.

1429   O cupbearer of the soul,

        go to the One who has a beautiful voice.

        He is the eternal melody.

        Listen to it, O falcon.

        Your heart beats to the sound of His drum.

        That Sultan is waiting for you.

        Now is the time to fly back to Him,

        the time for you to return.

1430   O source of joy and pleasure, stay here.

        Don't leave us.

        You were a grape of Absence.

        They made you into wine.

        O wine, don't become a grape again!

For the sake of the favors I have done for You,   1431
O Soul of souls, don't leave me.
You nursed me with the milk of Love.
I am drunk. Don't leave this baby of Love.
O Soul's parrot,
scatter sugar into this grateful cage.
Don't leave this land of sugar. Don't go.

Like your father who loves his son   1432
and gives advice all the time through quatrains,
recite quatrains in separation as well as in Union.
Collect a few quatrains to make an ode,
then recite more quatrains.

1433   O one who enjoys the tunes of doubt and suspicion,
all these are the imaginations
of your confused heart.
You are nothing,
and nothing could never be displayed to your eyes
as a something
better than this.

1434   O tears, go away from these sleepless eyes.
O fire, leave this burning heart.
O soul, this poor, humble body
is not your true dwelling place.
Leave it boldly. Look for glory and splendor.

O Beauty whose charming eyes 1435
have taken away my sleep,
where is the Water of Life, the sweets for the sleepless?
I have plunged into the river of Love.
Its water covers me in all six directions.[2]
But, I still can't see that water.

O heart, if you are aware of the words, 1436
"God is with you wherever you are,"[3]
why are you so confused?
If you forget these words,
you are attributing a partner to God.

---
[2]The material realm.
[3]Quran 57:4.

1437   O beautiful moon-faced One,

without You, I cried and cried like a cloud.

Without You, I had no joy when I looked at the Moon.

I took leave of my soul, because I had to sit without You.

And, I died from shame

because I was in such distress without You.

1438   O wise man, wise one, say something out loud.

It makes no difference if it is right or wrong.

Open the door to the rose garden and meadow.

Talk about the Friend like a drunken nightingale.

O drunken nightingale of the rose garden, 1439
singing songs gives drunkenness to the head
and peace to the soul.
O soul of the Universe, sing!
I am drunk and totally confused.
But, dear nightingale,
if you are able, sing something! Sing!

Don't reveal any secrets to non-confidants. 1440
Don't tell the story of the Beloved
to those denied access to the door of Love.
Don't talk substance with a stranger.
Don't talk with camels about anything except thorns.

1441 If you want to find You, hurry up and start searching.
Put yourself like a pot on top of Love's fire.
Boil up. Become exuberant.
Don't amble around aimlessly.
Come to a boil quickly.
Let Him burn you, ruin you,
so that you can find that pearl.

1442 The happiest man on Earth is a slave
of Your auspicious face.
The Universe is a poor beggar with a basket in its hand,
asking for Your favor.
The sky has been serving Your land for so many centuries,
yet it still can't pay for even one day of Your blessing.

There is a Turkish Beauty   1443
whose smile makes my heart rejoice,
whose scattered hair makes me ache with longing.
He took from me papers affirming my freedom,
then gave me papers stating that I had become His slave.

The one who becomes withered   1444
because of Your Love
cannot fit in the sky.
Once he becomes Your servant,
life turns into a servant for him.
I was biting my fingers when I entered through Your door.
But when I left, I was blissfully clapping my hands.

1445   I have felt the air of Your sorrow in my soul.

No, no. Souls are like particles in the sorrow of Your air.

Forms shine in the heart

because of the brilliance of the sorrow of Your air.

1446   Your beautiful smile, Your narcissus eyes, Your cheeks

are the remedies for sorrow and grief.

Do You know the reason for Your charm and beauty?

It is Your Love which breaks and burns hearts.

In Essence, Your soul and mine are the same. 1447
My soul and Yours are together as one.
Just for the sake of public understanding do I say,
"My soul, Your soul."
In fact, there is no "you" or "I" between us.

Ever since I first heard the melody of Your sorrow, 1448
I have been dancing like the particles of that sorrow.
O Beauty whose particles appear
in the light of sorrow's air,
out of all Your favors,
Your sorrow is the best and ultimate one.

1449 Your Love is the reason for joy.

O my moon-faced One,

Your fire is the source of life and longing.

If someone considers leaving,

Your scattered, unruly hair catches him

and brings him back again.

1450 I swear by Your face and Your being

that I know nothing about You.

You are unknowable.

You also have made me drunk,

taken my mind away and kept my hands empty.

But, I prostrate in gratitude

because of that drunkenness and emptiness

which come from You.

How can I consider the favors   1451
which have come from Your kindness,
when even more cries
have come from Your cruelty?
The cypress rose to the sky by being Your slave.
The rose ripped up its dress after being freed by You.

You brought my life as I knew it to an end.   1452
Life is passing anyway.
It would be best if it were to pass with You.
No, no. I said it wrong.
Life with You will never end!

1453   O my Beloved, even if all the Beauties leave, don't go.

O One who is so close to our souls,

who shares our troubles, don't go.

Offer wine. Fill up our glass. Smile sweetly.

O One who adorns the worlds and charms everyone,

O beautiful cupbearer, don't go.

1454   Beloved, do you feel any fondness towards me?

We are alone now, so tell me.

Do you love me or not?

Is there a place in your heart for me?

Yes or no?

As long as you tell the truth, say it.

Even if sugar envies your sweet smile, 1455
even if sultans are your slaves and servants,
if you are making this rotten world your Qibla,
you are dead, and people are licking your corpse.

If I had known my own value, 1456
I would not have fooled around with this dirty world.
I would have emptied myself from self
and ascended quickly.
I would have raised my head
above the ninth level of the sky.

1457 O moon-faced one, if you are in love with our Love,
free yourself from the bondage of the six dimensions.[4]
If you are looking for that Love,
move into the sea of our heart.
Why do you stop at the edge of the river?

1458 One day I said, "O my Beauty,
I am whole-heartedly Yours.
I haven't changed. I am the same.
I know without doubt that whatever I gamble,
I lose to You.
That is why I keep gambling.
It is the way I can be with You."

---

[4]The material realm.

Stay like a secret in my heart. Don't go away!   1459
Sit like a turban on my head. Don't go away!
You say to me, "I will go quickly,
but I will come back quickly."
Don't deceive me, O crafty beauty. Don't go away!

No one can diminish the one whom You have exalted.   1460
The soul which You have made low will rejoice forever.
Even the highest, most noble sky
kisses a hundred times a day
the feet which You have tied up with Your Love.

1461 I asked, "O beautiful One, where is Your house?"
He answered, "In your broken, ruined heart.
I am the Sun which shines into ruins.
O Love's drunk, destroy your heart.
Then, it will become My palace."

1462 My lips will not be opened for me without Your lips.
No word comes out of them without Yours.
God has locked the door of my heart and ordered,
"Don't open up your lips
without the lips of the Beloved."

We are the reason for the existence of the Universe,   1463
yet we are helpless in front of You.
We wonder about the soul,
and the soul wonders about You.
The Sun is Your star which keeps circling the Earth.
The Moon splits in two[5] because of Your Beauty.

Tell me, in either world, who is to me like You?   1464
Tell me, who is able to live in this world
without hope of You?
If I do something wrong and You punish me,
then tell me, what is the difference between me and You?

---

[5]Refers to the legend of the Prophet Muhammad splitting the Moon. Quran 54:1.

1465 O moon-faced Beauty,
I am drunk thanks to sugar from Your ruby lips.
I am so small in front of Your cypress-like stature.
My countenance has become pale
because of my longing for Your silvery body.
The color of my face has turned into gold.
O moon-faced One, don't give away this gold!

1466 O my friend, the ones who live in poverty
know what comes from the One
who brings the scent of Absence.
I swear to God that the sky and everyone in the sky
receive everything they have and everything they need
from Him.

If you run away from your soul, 1467
I will also run away from it.
If you run away from your heart, so will I.
If you become an arrow, I will become your bow.
It is not something of wonder
for an arrow to leave a bow.

You sang melodies with the Love of Eternity 1468
and became ignorant and stunned
by the confusion of Love.
You saved yourself from sorrows
by dying before your death.
You talked so much about His grief
that you became Him after all.

1469 Why are you wailing and complaining
about our troubles?
You should be grateful for Union.
Why are you running away from Me?
You might make Union very difficult.
Be afraid of that.
Be afraid of that.

1470 There is one who cannot sleep because of Your Love.
At night, ambergris from Your hair
is scattered all around.
In order to give peace to my heart,
the Painter of Eternity
draws the picture of the city of Tabriz[6] everywhere.

---

[6]A city in northwestern Iran from where Shams originated.

Hear the secrets from the parrots belonging to God. 1471
You are a fledgling parrot who knows that language.
Why are you so confused and stay sitting in your cage?
You belong in the sky.
Destroy your cage and fly!

I had this conversation with my Beauty: 1472
I first asked, "Have you grown weary of me?"
He answered, "Yes, because your soul has yet to give me
that thing which has a name
starting with the letter z."[7]
"Help!" I exclaimed. "What is the second letter?"
He answered, "r."

---

[7]Refers to the word zar which means gold in Farsi.

1473   As soon as He looks at me, I sacrifice myself.
His endearing behavior kills me.
He is like a full Moon,
a dancing branch causing me much agitation.
When He starts talking to me,
like that full Moon, I melt.

1474   I am here tonight. Next to me is a friend like me.
We sit right on the grass in the meadow.
There are appetizers, wine, candles and musicians
all displayed before us.
But, I wish you were here. Who cares about the rest?

Tonight, You are in the hands of Your slave. 1475
You will have a hard time getting out of these hands.
O tall beautiful cypress, unless You put Your chest
next to my burned, ruined heart,
You will not be able to escape from this slave.

You made me extremely agitated today. 1476
You took away all of my robes
which You Yourself had given me,
making me completely naked.
I couldn't keep up with You yesterday.
And, because I was asleep,
You drank the wine, then hid the portion
which fate had meant for me, Your slave.

1477 Last night, a charming Beauty came to me.
   I said, "Go away. Don't come tonight."
   While leaving, that Beauty said,
   "What kind of lover are you
   that the Kingdom comes to your door,
   but you don't open it?"

1478 Look at that face, fresh like a sugarcane field.
   Look at those beautiful eyes, beautiful like India.
   Cypresses form a line to look at that great stature.
   Even heroes like Rostam[8]
   are broken in the presence of those generous hands.

---

[8] A Persian king who became a legendary mythological hero with great powers.

When you fall in Love and become crazy-insane, 1479
you will be tied to the chain of saints.
Today, you are deprived of that chain,
because you are sober and immersed in life.

You always come late to Your lovers. 1480
When You do come, You quickly get tired of them.
Sometimes, You come as a gazelle;
at other times, You come as a lion.
Sometimes, You appear good-natured;
at other times, You appear sharp like a sword.

1481 If You were to serve that big glass

bargain-rate to everyone,

every particle in the Universe would be turned into Soul.

If You were to scatter sugar from Your sweet lips,

mountains would be moved

as if they were mere particles of dust.

1482 You are my soul, my only Beloved in both worlds.

You are my helper

and the answer to all my troubles and sorrows.

For me, there is no one but You in either world.

You offer me kindness and forgive my sin.

It would be nice if there were someone   1483
who could separate the good from the bad,
who could, without speaking or hearing others speak,
answer all questions,
who was that gardener
who gives out beautiful fruits to all of the guests
before they even ask.

The one who is not harmed by poison   1484
drinks poison like wine, O cupbearer.
When existence disappears, Absence comes.
The person who is saved from the self
drinks wine in the sea of abundance, cup after cup.

1485 O morning breeze,

  go to the place of my beautiful Beloved.

  If He receives you nicely, explain my situation.

  If He is in a bad mood,

  forget you saw my face and don't say anything.

1486 In the past, You comforted the oppressed

  and offered the wine of relief to the sufferer.

  But now, that wine which he drank in the eternal past

  has been forgotten.

  If You don't give it to him anymore,

  why are You giving him the memory of it?

Whatever happens, the future will come. 1487
You know this.
In fact, you know the difference
between the one in the basket
and the one in eternity.
I say this during the day
so that it can be remembered at night.
I say it in the night, because you yourself are aware of it.

One who is drunk even when he seems sober 1488
is the most pleasant and gracious
when he is deeply drunk.
He may sometimes hide his drunkenness,
because Love's plectrum strikes
sometimes on the high end of the strings
and sometimes on the low.

1489   The One[9] who yelled, "I am the Truth,"

        has been hanging on Love's gallows ever since.

        The one who casts spells with his eyes

        keeps beating himself in thousands of ways,

        all out of longing for You.

1490   A gazelle runs when it sees a dog.

        A rider gallops when he is attacked.

        They are exerting themselves to the extreme,

        believing their salvation is to be found in

        that racing pulse.

---

[9]Hallaj Mansur, a famous Sufi martyred for his beliefs (858-922 CE).

My face was very pale before today.   1491
My heart was crying, crying, crying.
I was crazy like Majnun.[10]
But, something just happened to me.
Now everything in the past
has become ordinary and forgotten.

O Hodja,[11] tell me, are you free or bound?   1492
Who would buy
such a rebellious and disorderly slave?
O one who raises his hands to pray, tell me,
who raises your hands?
Who gives you the desire to pray?
Those desires are not yours. They are His.

---
[10]In the famous Arabic love story, Majnun loses his mind because of the intensity of his love for Layla.
[11]A title meaning teacher or scholar, or in this case, wise fool. Nasreddin Hodja is Turkey's (and perhaps all of Islam's) most famous trickster.

1493 O gentle hearts who are sowing the seeds of loyalty
and scattering pearls of joy on black soil,
wherever you are, you know my situation.
Please, don't leave me in the land of separation!

1494 O Sultan, are you remembering the throne?
Are you remembering the Sultan of sultans?
O imperial tent, your flaps have been dancing.
Are you remembering that the wind
can change you from one form to another?

When a strong, energetic body   1495
is afflicted by troubles from You,
when it is stained with Your Karbala's blood,[12]
when it becomes idle, existing only for You,
my God, what work could that one possibly do?

O heart, you have seen signs of the dawn of a new day   1496
in the middle of the night.
Do you know any sincere lover with a good reputation?
You keep yelling, "I am burnt!" Don't!
Do you know any burnt one who is still raw?

---

[12]Refers to the murder of the Prophet Muhammad's grandson, Imam Husayn, in the Battle of Karbala in 680 CE.

1497   O humans who are better than the

Moon and moonlight,

you have been created from water and mud,

but you are better than that!

Why are you stuck in the mud?

O drunks of the tavern,

you are submerged in a whirlpool.

Why do you sleep day and night?

Wake up!

1498   O pure and beautiful people

who keep searching all over the world,

what are you searching for?

The Beauty you seek is inside of you.

That is the only place you will ever find that Beloved.

How amazing are those who are killed by their own souls. 1499
Such a thing is not widely known, but, in fact,
it is the Water of Life which kills them.
Or, if they appear in public,
then it is the people who kill them.
Or, if they hide in Love,
then it is Love which kills them.

Do not change the melody of the heart, 1500
so that the pleasure of that melody will not disappear.
Do not look at anything except the heart,
so that its sweetness will not disappear.
Your ecstasy is like paradise,
so do not give up your drunkenness.
Stay on the journey,
so that paradise will not disappear.

1501   There is a secret in our hearts which keeps turning.
It is the reason for the movement of every creature.
Even this whirling sky depends on it.
This secret doesn't distinguish head from feet.
It keeps turning without head or feet.

1502   First, the One who charmed you with His Beauty
arrived, taking your mind away and confusing you.
Next, He entered your eyes as a salve.
Then, He watched His own Beauty through your eyes.

You shouldn't cling to your mistake. 1503
You should let it run its course.
But, you do need a key from God's grace
to open the lock of such an incident.

This drunk is intoxicated with a different kind of wine. 1504
His jar is empty,
but that wine keeps whirling in his head.
So, don't whip him, O muhtesib.[13]
The more you do, the more drunk he will become.

---

[13][Arabic] A supervisor of bazaars and trade in medieval Islamic countries whose duty was to ensure that public business was conducted according to Sharia [religious law], which includes the prohibition of wine-drinking.

1505   It is amazing that the Beloved is contained in my heart.
Souls of a thousand bodies fit in this flesh.
One grain grows into thousands of harvests.
Hundreds of universes fit in the eye of a needle.

1506   Something is turning around in my head tonight.
My heart has become a bird, circling in the air.
Every particle of my body is turning separately.
I wonder. Is the Beloved turning around devotion?

The shout of that drunk is coming from the sky. 1507
He is coming with yells and cries and screams.
Thanks to all that clamor,
the soul and the world have become exuberant.
They both are coming from that other realm.

The blessing of His Union will never hurt you. 1508
I swear on your soul
that His Union will never trouble you.
The Beloved only scares you to make you courageous.
The Beloved wants you to fill your heart with Him.
Once your heart is filled, evil eyes can never touch you.

1509 What are truth and falsehood

in front of God's light?

What are sweetness and bitterness

in front of God's grace?

When even the Sun is ashamed in front of His light,

what is the use of those other little lights

remaining in the sky?

1510 Do me a favor. Smile at this slave,

and I will smile back at You in return.

I am weeping bitterly

so that my bloody tears will be wine for You,

so that my burning heart can be Your kabob.

Get up. Don't be lethargic.   1511
The Beloved has announced
that your trials are over
and you are free.
My own sleep has died.
As long as graveyard dirt covers it,
may your life be long.

There are remedies which are worse than troubles.   1512
There are riches which can make you
poor and destitute.
True fear of God will make you fervent,
unlike that earthly fear which turns fervors cold.

1513   You need to suffer longer with that broken heart.
Your status and distinction depend on it.
If you are a human being, get along with people.
If you are an angel, ascend to the sky.

1514   There was light in the sky from Your fire.
There was water in the Earth's rivers from Your sea.
That water was a mirage. That fire was lightening.
Since no traces remain,
perhaps they were both just a dream.

My moon-faced One asked me if I had seen the Moon.   1515
I exclaimed, "Yes! How amazing!
The Moon is asking about a moon!"
He responded,
"I am asking about the month of the Moon."
"Oh!" I exclaimed. "The Eid is asking about an Eid!"[14]

I am tired of the rubies which turn out to be turquoise.   1516
I am tired of the loves which last only three days.
I am tired of this bankrupt kingdom.
I am tired of the Eid which makes us part with fasting.

---

[14]The Islamic lunar month of Ramadan ends with the appearance of the new Moon and is celebrated with the religious holiday known as Eid.

1517 I am tired of the water

which hasn't been turned into fire by Love,

of the hair which doesn't become wild

and scattered by Love,

and of my Beloved who is nice and beautiful,

but who has decided to stop being disruptive and unruly!

1518 The words coming from my mouth are not mine.

Although I talk with His words,

I am not aware of them.

The poison and sugar come from my heart.

What does my heart know about the future,

about which words would be suitable and proper?

Feet cannot be like the head. They cannot lead us.　1519
And, that chosen Beauty cannot be unruly.
He is a true spring of the Water of Life.
The Water of Life cannot be like fire.

This lover's sick, broken heart has come back again.　1520
It went out on its feet,
but came back on its head,
suffering so much all for sugar.
In the end, like a fly,
it lost its patience and came back again to sugar.

1521   I shot an arrow up into the sky,
but the arrow fell down
and hit a believer right in the heart.
He cursed and asked,
"Was this a secret desire of yours
turned into an accident?"
I answered, "No. The arrow I shot
was God's desire turned into an accident."

1522   An arrow was shot into the air
from the bow of the rebab player.
It passed through my body's shield
and made a direct hit on my heart.
Look at what penetrates into Essence.
Hear the sound of the rebab
which silences all other sounds.

You are soul, 1523
and all living people feel the grief of Your soul.
All are concerned about their possessions,
but when united with You,
they know they are attached to gold
and silently endure even the blows of Your sword.

I searched for my soul in the sea. 1524
A coral came into view,
but then hid itself under the foam.
I started my journey
on that narrow path into the darkness of my heart.
I walked and walked until, finally, a desert appeared.

1525   O Beloved, the heat of Your Love's fire
has reached the extreme!
There is nothing but complaining left for me.
Please, if You don't want to listen to my wailing,
come to me at early dawn,
because the troubles of Your Love
have passed all boundaries.

1526   In my soul there were different desires
which kept yelling and screaming in Your air.
But, after I caught a fragrance from the wine of Love,
I threw myself like a dead leaf into Love's wind.

My soul has a beautiful Beloved.   1527
It lives, like a salamander,[15] in the fire of that Beloved.
O cupbearer, serve me the wine of my Beloved's lips.
That wine
leaves such a strange drunkenness in my head.

What a soul it is which sees and admires Your work!   1528
What an eye and heart they are
which have been hunted by You.
If thorns were to grow at the head of my grave,
they would also long for You, love You!

---

[15] A mythological lizard which can live in fire.

1529   My heart set forth on a journey

and kept advancing until it reached a desert.

Even the roads have wondered

how it was possible for me to come this far.

If Majnun[16] lost his mind for Love

and climbed a mountain, what would be new in that?

I am also Majnun, but the difference is this:

hundreds of mountains of sorrows have come to me.

1530   When that concealed Beauty

comes out from behind the curtain,

every secret throws its dress away, becoming naked.

The greedy person gives away all of his goods.

The rock becomes a mine which scatters jewels.

---

[16]In the famous Arabic love story, Majnun loses his mind because of the intensity of his love for Layla.

Since the day of Union with my Beloved   1531
is not in sight,
I started thinking that I should give up this Love
little by little.
"That is impossible," said my heart,
and bent its head down.
Even so, I saw how it was secretly chuckling.

Since my eyesight is gone,   1532
what is the use of Your salve?
Since my heart has been squeezed of all blood,
what is the use of Your loyalty?
Since my heart and soul
have been burned out by Your sorrow,
what is the use of Your sweet, calming words?

1533 Can a heart which has fallen in Love
still look at this world?
Impossible!
In fact, there is nothing in this world worth seeing
except Love.
I am tired of the eyes which,
on the day of death,
look at the soul instead of looking at Love.

1534 Heaven forbid that a lover would ever be forsaken by You.
He should not be separated from Your countenance.
All my explanations are of no use in that
lover's presence.
They are just like worthless stories shared
at a dinner feast.

God knows that I have become the dirt under your feet,   1535
so it should be that you sit in front of me.
If you are taken away from me, I will keep praying
until there is mercy and you sit before me again.

I want that dust which is coming from Your air.   1536
I want that dust from the place where You stand
to get into my eyes.
I enjoy the suffering which comes from You,
because that is what allows me
to catch the fragrance of Your faithfulness.

1537 I pleaded in front of that Sultan of sultans
who gave the Moon to the Earth
to give everything to you.
You know that that Sultan knows best.
So, He promised to hand you
the wealth of the heart, the land of faith
and the knowledge of the sage.

1538 I hope you have pleasant days and fulfill all your desires.
May only joy and pleasure accompany you at Fil-abad.[17]
May the One who created pain and troubles
save you from them
when you decide to live at Fil-abad!

---

[17]A palace west of Konya, Turkey.

When the image of Your face appeared before my eyes,   1539
my sleep turned its head and ran.
Now, I am asking You to mete out justice to Your image.
My sleep returned, holding
the hem of Your robe for protection.
But, as soon as it saw Your image again, it died!

What a beautiful habit Muhammad[18] has.   1540
He never leaves us alone on dark evenings.
He keeps playing the rebab until morning.
When he feels sleepy,
he cuts the throat of his sleep.

---

[18]Muhammad Bahaeddin [Sultan Veled], Rumi's son (1227-1312 CE).

1541   Do you know why that Sufi is eating so much?
It is because he eats only one time a day.
Let him eat roses for a moment.
He eats thorns like a camel
from the Beloved's mountain of sorrow,
and who knows how long that will last!

1542   I still hold the hem of the robe of Your greatness.
The drunkenness from the wine You have served
still remains in my head.
You said to me, "Appear as you are."
But, it is impossible to appear as I am.

If I look at the Beloved, He becomes bashful.   1543
If I don't, my heart is tormented.
Stars glitter in each drop of sweat on His face.
Without that, my heart becomes dim and muddled.

O my Beloved, when I worship You,   1544
I prostrate toward my fortune, my glory.
And, whenever I pray to You,
it is my soul deep inside of me which is begging.

1545   He is in the meaning, not in the words.
        He is in the heart, not on the tongue.
        He is the Essence of the Universe, but not the Universe.
        He is neither in Absence nor existence.

1546   You possess a hidden pearl
        which fills thousands of oceans.
        If you want to find it, don't act silly.
        If you follow a donkey, you'll end up in a barn.
        Look for that pearl instead inside of your heart.

To sacrifice thousands of hearts and souls for Love   1547
is not enough!
What is soul? It isn't even worth being mentioned!
One who journeys on the way of Love
must sacrifice hundreds of souls at every step
and never look back.

One has to be loyal to Your Love.   1548
Reaching You is only a dream now,
but it must become a reality.
This wounded heart is Your slave,
serving You well at Your temple.
But, I need something even better.

1549   Even the most skillful mind
is unable to think of Your Love
and fall asleep at the same time.
Some lovers who long for You
catch fever and sleep in that fever's fire.
I am a lover without eyes, without heart.
How could one think I could sleep?
Both of my eyes have become blood.
How could one think blood could sleep?

1550   When Your Love takes its place
in the mind of the firmament,
trouble fills the world clear up to the skies.
When Your Love catches the world's soul,
the world turns into one soul
and neither up nor down remains.

If there would be more sorrow and mourning   1551
in the houses of the disloyal ones,
then the number of disloyal ones
would be diminished in this world.
As you can see, no one looks after me except loyal sorrow.
Thousands of thanks and praises to that sorrow!

Harsh words are coming from Your lips,   1552
but those words are as valuable as rubies,
because they hold the essence of fire.
You say such harsh words to attract hearts.
And, You succeed, because Your words
are like a light breeze
coming from that beautiful, fragrant rose garden.

1553 When I was next to my beloved, I said to my heart,

"Don't go anywhere. My beloved is here!"

My beloved coyly responded,

"Who is this heart of yours

that it comes or goes on your command?"

1554 You are the sultan of my heart.

Rule like a sultan.

Torture me as you wish.

I don't mind. It is your right.

You have a glass full of wine in your hand.

Offer it to me.

Then, do whatever you wish.

I am in love with you 1555
despite the fact that you are always breaking my heart,
and I will endure.
But, for even one day, don't you feel ashamed
when you see my heart so wounded?

There is no one like that Sultan in either world. 1556
No one is His peer,
not secretly, not openly, not above, not below.
Every arrow is shot from His bow.
Every wise and celebrated word comes from Him.

1557   While he is talking,

His forehead and cheeks turn into fire.

His languid eyes become reddish.

The torrent of blood

takes away his patience and sensibilities.

O Love who allows words to flow,

have him start talking!

1558   "I saw the fermentation of Love's wine jar

because of You.

I became mature wine because of You."

"No, no," I said. "That is wrong.

I am just water. You are the wine.

I disappear after mixing with You."

Why all this anger and greed 1559
while in the sea of kindness?
Why the stealing of water
in a time when there is so much of it
and all of it is so exceptionally sweet?
And, why steal from a friend?
A fish never saves water as treasure.
It needs that water to exist.
While in the sea, it doesn't worry about such things.

A fish never stores water, 1560
O wise man,
because he isn't in a strange land.
He is in the sea.[19]

---

[19]The first two lines of this quatrain are missing from the original text.

1561 I can't keep my eyes off of His bow-like eyebrow.
   I put my soul like a target in front of His arrows.
   Every wound lifts up a curtain.
   When He steps aside, I keep begging for more.

1562 If you want to caress His curly hair,
   why do you hesitate with deep thoughts?
   Plunge into it
   and look for the light there.

He is a secret rose garden   1563
which so many trees and bushes are concealing.
He appears in hundreds of different shapes,
but He is the only One.
He is an ocean without coasts which covers everything.
One wave from this ocean
becomes hundreds of waves in every soul.

I cannot talk about the thing   1564
which happened between us last night,
nor can I write about it.
Pieces of my shroud will tell this story
at the time I depart from this old world.

1565 When I saw you last night,

      you wanted us to be separated.

      You tormented me, saying, "Go away. Leave me alone."

      Today, I am separated from my soul

      and washing my face with the blood of loneliness.

1566 I saw You, O Beauty. Don't cover Your face.

      Don't drink wine without us.

      O One who is the eye and light of lovers,

      don't listen if an evil one gossips about You.

Last night the Beloved satisfied us   1567
with hundreds of spells of Love.
But then, He opened my heart.
When He saw blood inside, He ordered,
"He is not yet cooked.
Throw him back into the fire."

Get the seal of the sultanate from that Sultan of soul.   1568
Rule everywhere, everyone from the Moon to the fish.
O one who reels with amazement at beauty,
say, "Tabriz,"[20] and then take whatever you wish.

---

[20] A city in northwestern Iran from where Shams originated.

1569   I was captivated by the drunks and became a drunk.

        I surrendered to their might

        and gave up my mind.

        I became a crazy one

        in order to be admitted into Love's asylum.

1570   I am Your insane one, Your drunk.

        My drunkenness is not from wine or opium.

        It is from You.

        Don't expect good manners from me.

        My exuberance causes hundreds of rivers to overflow.

        The skies are amazed at my whirling.

I have so much longing   1571
that even the sky cannot stand it.
Majnun[21] would not be able to experience
such exuberance, even in his dreams.
This exaltation is only a small bit of the Beloved's,
so imagine what there is in His heart.

If your hands get tired of serving the Beloved,   1572
use your feet.
If your feet get tired, yell and scream.
If you lose your voice, use your head.
In other words,
be faithful every moment to the Beloved.

---

[21]In the famous Arabic love story, Majnun loses his mind because of the intensity of his love for Layla.

1573   If I am wounded and dying in the war for your Love,
I won't cry or complain so as not to bother you.
At the stab of your sharp gaze,
I will smile like a rose and die smiling.

1574   Everywhere, Iraq, Damascus, Nuristan,[22]
all are now illuminated by the light of Your face.
Be a friend of Munkar and Nakir,[23]
so that the ones who are buried in the graveyard
may start clapping their hands and dance.

---

[22]A region in Afghanistan.
[23]Two angels who test the faith of the dead in their graves.

In this world, there is no one except Him.   1575
Apparent, concealed, beautiful, ugly,
there is no one except Him.
Every arrow comes from Him.
Every word comes from Him.

He is a secret rose garden   1576
which so many trees and bushes are concealing.
He appears in hundreds of different shapes,
but He is the only One.
He is an ocean without coasts which covers everything.
One wave from this ocean
becomes hundreds of waves in every soul.

1577   We are Love's lazy ones, lying on the ground.
       Only His grace made the Earth into a saddle horse,
       so that lovers like us, like the Ashāb al kahf[24]
       could be carried in our sleep
       to the top of the sky.

1578   We are beautiful.
       If you follow our custom,
       if you make friends with us and no one else,
       you will also be adorned and become beautiful.
       Don't remain a drop.
       Annihilate your self.
       Turn yourself into an ocean.

---

[24][Arabic] Companions of the Cave. Refers to the story of a group of up to seven youths who hid in a cave outside Ephesus (approx. 250 CE) to escape religious persecution, re-emerging 300 years later. Quran 18:9-26.

The whole Universe is My lover. 1579
All who need help and who offer it need My remedies.
The Sun and the heavens are My slaves,
revolving around Me.
Onlookers of both worlds are absorbed in seeing Me.

Your heroes 1580
who have abandoned certain religious beliefs
are in the circle of Kun feyakun,[25]
and the heart is a dot in the center of that circle,
which is bigger than the throne of God.
When this dot of trouble is consumed,
you will escape the Universe and ascend to Union.

---

[25][Arabic] When Allah commands the Universe to "Be [kun], it becomes [feyakun]." Quran 2:117.

1581 When I see You smile, I smile, too.
My soul is a slave of Your smile
which You make without mouth or lips.
It is sad that no one else can see it,
but it is completely concealed
from the eyes of the people.

1582 It is so nice to move from one place to another,
not to freeze, but to flow like running water.
Yesterday has gone.
The stories of yesterday are also gone.
Today, we must say something new.

Call that musician an illiterate one.   1583
He cannot read from the book of the heart.
Tell him, "If odes and verses hide their faces from you,
look at our faces and read their beauty from them."

You are the light of my heart,   1584
the peace and comfort of my soul.
You create trouble, and You are the trouble.
At the same time,
You and Your trouble are the remedy.
They ask me,
"Where are the signs and evidence of the Beloved?"
But, the lack of signs and evidence
is the sign and evidence of the Beloved!

1585 Be aware: it is a custom

of those two beautiful drunken eyes

to make amorous gestures.

In this way, they create doubt and suspicion.

Cast out sleepiness from your head.

Every moment, pound upon it.

With every breath separate wheat grains from chaff.

1586 I don't want to be alone!

Either my charmer or my heart should be with me,

but neither one is!

O my charmer, don't come without your heart.

One heart is better for me

than a hundred heartless charmers.

O my God, what a great, divine being is this heart! 1587
It constantly searches for the Beloved,
suffering through all kinds of troubles.
It has put its head on His threshold so many times
that the ground of that threshold says,
"This heart has a thousand faces."

O one who is peerless in beauty, you are in my soul. 1588
Do you regret the promise you made to me?
When you loved me, you asked, "Who are you?"
But, you are leaving me today without asking who I am.

1589 When you obtain an unpierced pearl,
   heads will be brought together
   and secrets will be revealed.
   For you, this barn which is called the world
   will be forgotten.
   In fact, you will realize,
   once you are drunk and contentedly sleeping,
   that this world isn't worth a grain of barley.

1590 Don't go after the crazy one who runs away.
   Let him go. Don't be bothered.
   The one who is annihilated by the glass of Love
   is insane, out of existence
   and cannot be contained by ordinary chains.

The way to Union is not what you think it is.   1591
This Earth is not the realm of the soul,
a soul which you have sadly forsaken.
On your way, you passed a fountain,
that fountain from which Khidr[26]
drank the Water of Life.
But, you filled it with dirt and plugged it all up.

O moon-faced One, You are the atonement for every sin.   1592
You are the rope to pull the soul's Joseph from the well.
No, You are better than that!
You are the guide on the road to heaven.
O moon-faced One,
You are the key to thousands of suns.

---

[26] A legendary Godsend who attained immortality by drinking from the Water of Life and who comes to help those in moments of extreme distress.

1593   O friend who has left his friend,

       it was so nice when the heart had the benefit

       of being next to you.

       But, you turned your face away from this friend,

       and now the enemy is joyfully bidding for his boots.

1594   O respectable religious elder,

       you have become an idol worshiper.

       Do not live for pleasure. Annihilate yourself!

       Do not grieve if things become tight and hard.

       Keep drinking from that intoxicating, wide-open jar.

Beloved, You are nothing but joy and grace. 1595
How can I yell and scream when You are inside of me?
The taste and pleasure of the world is in Your lips.
Yet, You are not a part of this world!

O friend who caressed me with kindness 1596
and made me happy,
now you are looking for excuses to get rid of me.
If you do the same to everyone,
you surely do not know the value of friendship.

1597   O friend, don't cast a spell on me.

It is eating up everything great and small for me.

I swear by your heart and soul,

I can create a spell so powerful

that my warm breath will tie running water into a knot!

1598   O beautiful One,

people have dipped their bread in Your salt.

They have put their brands on Your horse.

It is sad when,

after inciting troubles among the people,

such a silver-statured Beauty, hidden like the soul,

leaves for the mine.

O One whose face glitters like fire, 1599
how long will You consume me like this?
You have already burned me
a hundred times, in a hundred ways.
You ask,
"Why are you closing your eyes to My face?"
I am not.
You never taught me to do anything like that.

The world is beautiful and joyful because of You. 1600
You are the source of pleasure and happiness,
while we are only one part of the thirty.[27]
You are the Sun who illuminates this world.
Not even thousands of stars and the Moon could do that.

---

[27]Very possibly, a reference to the thirty birds who successfully reach the Simurgh [the King of Birds] after their long, hard journey in the Sufi allegory, *The Conference of the Birds*, by Farid ud-Din Attar.

1601   The soul which could understand
neither His Arabic nor His Farsi
saw the cup of wine which had not yet been tasted.
With God's grace, the sea must become exuberant
in order for the soul to see its ability to strive.

1602   My stone-hearted Beloved returned.
He broke my heart into a hundred pieces.
I was at the assembly, helpless before Him.
His Love seized me, and made me cry like a harp.

Listen to this advice from a crazy one of Love: 1603
if you consort with strangers,
you will become a stranger,
so make all strangers leave the house of your heart.
Then, like the house of the honey bee,
your heart will be filled
with hundreds of combs of honey.

You laugh as you find excuses. 1604
You set up traps and scams in your own home.
O one who turns his face to the sky like an innocent one,
you can split a piece of hair into forty pieces
with all kinds of tricks and deceits.

1605 The sky greets me, saying,
"O one whose bewildered head turns like mine!"
But, the sky and its friends are the only ones
which whirl around bewildered.
The one who has a lofty yearning is not bewildered.
In fact, he is a support for each revolving sky.

1606 O smart, learned man, do you know what the night is?
It is the time of solitude for lovers,
isolation from strangers,
especially tonight
when the moon-faced Beloved
is in the house of my heart.
I am drunk.
The moon which walks silently around the sky is in love,
and the night is crazy-insane.

If you are not a thorn, come to the garden with a rose. 1607
If you are not a stranger, come close to us.
Unless you are a snake,
don't show us a face full of poison.
Unless you are a picture on the wall,
look at this page
and understand the meaning of this writing.

Your long, thick, dark curls 1608
have blocked out the light of every single one of my days.
Anything Your curls touch comes back to life,
because they are so full of life and soul.
Those long curls will drag on the floor,
but I am never allowed to touch them.

1609　The one who sees Him through the heart
becomes ecstatic.
Blind are the ones who are lost in thought.
Hundreds of branches have scattered roses and flowers
from the Land of Absence to you.
Why do you cut down the tree of contentment?

1610　We are in a season
which is as auspicious as the Beloved's Union.
As the body dies, the lamp of the heart becomes alive.
When lightning strikes, clouds start crying,
which makes the garden smile.

Even when you are with everyone, 1611
you are lonely if you cannot find Me in your heart.
If you are in solitude and think about Me,
you are with everyone.
Don't just be attached to others.
Leave yourself. Become the others.
There are times
when you are a slave of your deceit and anger.

I asked, "What should I do?" 1612
He answered, "O poor helpless man,
just do something.
You keep repeating,
'What should I do? What should I do?'
Unless you do something,
you will always stay in the same place and go nowhere."

1613   I said, "O Beloved, You are the wine. I am the glass.
       I am the lifeless body. You are my soul.
       Come now and open the door of Your kindness."
       He said, "Be silent.
       Only an insane one
       keeps his door open to someone all the time."

1614   I said, "My longing for You has made me crazy-insane.
       When I sleep, I have dreams
       of being in chains put on by You."
       He said, "Be silent.
       What kind of nonsense are you mumbling about?
       Insane and asleep? Don't be ridiculous, my gifted one!"

We are brave men, dwelling in a narrow valley. 1615
Lions are passing by, and so are wolves.
But, we have merged with Absence
like a ewe nursing her lamb.

Accept fasting as a beggar's basket in hand. 1616
Don't let it go.
Let fasting be a way for you to beg on the way of God,
so that God will award you with the Water of Life
and your thirst will be satisfied.
Fasting resembles a fragile jar. Don't break it!

1617 I said, "Night has come, O my moon-faced Beauty."
He answered me
by talking about the Moon and the night.
"There is a time for the Moon
when it turns its face away from the Sun.
At that time, the Sun becomes dark and night comes."

1618 I was drinking wine with a cheerful, vivacious beauty.
Sleep took me away from myself
before I realized the desire of my heart.
When I woke up from the sleep of drunkenness,
the beauty was gone, the candle was extinguished
and the cupbearer was fast asleep.

Now is the time of patience. 1619
The month of fasting has come.
For a couple of days, don't talk about a bowl and pitchers.
Sit around the table of the sky
in order to free the thread of the soul
from the cotton ball.

My heart is in the service 1620
of Your beautiful ruby lips.
Its drunkenness comes from Your drunken eyes.
If a thorn bush grows on my grave,
it will still be crying out,
crying out for You.

1621   My heart sings all about Your springtime.

My soul praises Your tulip garden.

If a thorn bush grows on my grave,

it will still be crying out,

crying out for You.

1622   I hit that heart-catching beauty,

the one who soothed me, who gave his heart to me.

I hit that beloved whom I had kissed and caressed.

I became so insane

that I hit that friend who had given life and joy to me.

Last night, the sky drank wine from Your Moon. 1623
The world drank wine
from Your fountain of the Water of Life.
Whoever and whatever has the strength of living
has drunk wine from Your Water of Life.

The one who rides Love's horse 1624
is viewed by other people as crazy.
But for us, crazy is the one
who can recognize God's lover,
the one who recognizes Truth.

1625   Your eyes were casting charms yesterday.

   The brightness of Your face reflected the sky.

   While Your sun-face was showing

   in between the shadows of Your hair,

   my soul kept dancing like a dust particle in Your light.

1626   The peace of my soul

   keeps turning around my heart and my soul.

   I grow like a tree from the earthly ground of my body,

   because the Water of Life is turning around me.

When Your love makes me crazy, 1627
I will do things which even the devil wouldn't do.
Not even the pen of the Vizier of the Sultan's Dîvân
could write such commands on my heart as You do.

O beauty, your hair has caused even practical people 1628
to fall down to the ground.
It lays so beautifully on your arms and neck
and smells like ambergris.
Do not be disturbed by these passionate words.
Your beautiful hair might become jumbled and tangled
and, like those practical people,
fall down and touch the ground.

1629 My dungeon is superior to freedom.

My curse is sweeter than sugar.

My sword's strike is better than life.

My ruby is more beautiful than purity.

1630 There is a secret which the Beloved

is saying secretly with the tip of His tongue.

He is the One who knows the reason for our being.

Alas, I know about the hundreds of mills

in all the right places

which are all idle because of the lack of water.

The bird which is raised in the garden of the master   1631
becomes obstinate and, at the same time, drunk and coy.
But, if it wants to guide the master,
it will be caught,
because the pride of early flight will have deceived it.

Good news for all seekers: 1632
The One whom they have been searching for has come!
O lovers, yell and shout with joy.
Your Beloved has come!
Job is relieved of troubles!
The Joseph of thousands of Jacobs has come!

1633   How beautiful does my Beloved look from a distance!
He keeps playing with His sleeve like a child.
Then, He calls me to sit next to Him and,
as He opens His arms,
He captures the bird of my heart like a falcon!

1634   How happy is the person who sees moonlight
on the face of the Beloved!
How nice it is getting drunk with wine
by the hand of the benevolent cupbearer!
Tears keep running from the lover's eyes.
Sleep doesn't come,
because it is afraid of the torrent
which would carry it away.

This night is filled with Love   1635
like the hearts of lovers
which are concealed from both good and evil eyes.
There is a secret journey
which I am taking with my bleeding heart.
On this night Love is saying,
"The time has come. Be ready to return to your origin."

I have caused all the creatures   1636
of the Earth and the sky
to feel more restless than they have ever felt before.
Not even hundreds of Majnuns.[28]
have ever experienced such intense exuberance.
I experience it all because Your soul is my soul.
Ask your own soul,
"Who could ever complain
about the burden of his soul?"

---

[28]In the famous Arabic love story, Majnun loses his mind because of the intensity of his love for Layla.

1637   Morning has come. The time for daylight has arrived.

For those who stayed awake all night,

the time of separation has arrived.

The eye which was our night guard has fallen asleep.

The time for desiring sugar has arrived.

1638   My mind has left a hundred times

and returned a hundred times.

How long have I kept drinking wine

from the cup of lovers?

I have ceased from activity as well as from idleness.

Where will this business finally come to an end?

The lover should drink wine   1639
for as long as he is on the road.
He drinks wine to get rid of reason and modesty.
So, why should I drink wine?
What would wine do to me?
There is no reason left in my mind.

Love is such a thing that it intoxicates people.   1640
Love is such a thing that it gives joy and exuberance.
We are not born from mothers.
Love delivered us.
Hundreds of blessings,
hundreds of bravos for that mother.

1641 At first, You didn't offer Divine Love.

Adam covered this void

with the melodies of the zurna.

That zurna drank the wine of Your lips for so long

that it became drunk and began crying with joy.

1642 Eid has come,

that Eid which will get an Eid gift from You.

It has brought grain from Your Eid crescent Moon.

It is turning its face to that Moon.

But, it cannot take that new crescent Moon

to its home.

Sorrow doesn't come close to the Sultan's slaves. 1643
There is no room for it among good fortune and grace.
There is something above joy and pleasure,
and that thing turns around in their heads.

Because of Love, my neck which was straight like an alif 1644
became bent like a jîm.[29]
The beauty of the Universe doubles itself
wherever You are.
Since my heart perceives the part which appears,
I run after the rest.

---

[29]Two alphabetic letters shared by the Arabic and Persian alphabets.

1645 Nothing, not even rose or basil had helped me.
I said to myself,
"Be silent. His bow doesn't match your shield."
Then, I was shot from that bow
like a three-winged arrow.
Even so, I reached the summit of His sorrow
without the help of those three wings!

1646 An infidel is the one
who hasn't become crazy with longing
after seeing You.
The one who doesn't give his life to You is dead.
I wouldn't even call universal reason reasonable
if it didn't become insane and disgraced
in front of You.

Since I have met my Beloved, 1647
my heart and my eyes
have become mere useless trifles.
My eyes will keep crying out my heart's blood
until that Beloved embraces me.

How does the Sun illuminate the darkness of night? 1648
His fiery heart gets rid of sleep.
Tears come, but sleep doesn't,
because it is afraid of the torrent of tears
which would carry it away.

1649   If you become unjust and hurt people,
       what is the value of your promise to God?
       What is the use of honey after you have served poison?
       It is good to work for people.
       What is the value of helping only yourself?

1650   When a man dies, they carry his body over their heads.
       But, when he is alive, their intention is to end his life.
       I said, "They made me a friend of the rowdies."
       "No, no," He answered,
       "They call you the town drunk."

If I suffer through His Love silently,   1651
my heart becomes tight out of longing for Him.
If I share the secrets of my heart,
jealous people fight with me.
If I protect the glass of my heart
to keep it from being shattered against a rock,
He says, "Are you tired of My Love for you?"

Wouldn't it be nice if you didn't try to avoid me?   1652
Wouldn't it be nice
if you stopped playing the farewell game with me?
My lips are dry and my eyes wet
because of being separated from you.
Wouldn't it be nice if you had pity on them?

1653   Summer is hot, bringing the steady heat of an oven.
When You come suddenly, I feel like summer is here.
That's how much warmth I feel.
Although it doesn't last forever, winter is cold.
When You promise to come and don't,
that feels like everlasting cold to me.

1654   When sleep overwhelms you,
I don't allow anyone to wake you up.
But, when Love shakes you like an apple tree,
it blows your sleep away
like the wind blows away dry leaves.

One who has boarded a sailing boat 1655
sees that trees are moving on the shore.
It is like that.
We are passing by through the world.
But, we think that the world is passing us.

I said, "O Beloved, it is so painful! 1656
Your troubles are increasing every moment!"
He said, "How wonderful
that you have reached the point of suffering
from My troubles."
I said, "My heart is bleeding.
Blood is pouring from my eyes!"
He said, "How blessed you are!
This has not happened to anyone else."

1657   I said,

       "My heart has become accustomed to His troubles.

       How nice if I were to get some more."

       O lover, come to your senses.

       Open your arms and embrace His troubles.

       Once you do and then you open your eyes,

       you will see that His troubles have become Him.

1658   I asked, "My heart is so small

       that it can't even be seen among the visible.

       How can Your big sorrow fit into it?"

       He answered, "Look at your eye. It is also small.

       But, don't big things fit in there?"

You said, "Tell," 1659
but words cannot reveal that secret.
How could a tongue deliver a secret of Love?
Nothing in the whole Universe could ever verbalize it.
It is impossible to talk about the breath
which was mixed with the dust of Adam.[30]

They say, "There will be a beautiful paradise. 1660
Clear, ruby-red wine will be served there
by black-eyed virgins."
But, we have already been blessed with that wine
and we are already sitting with the Beloved.

---

[30]Quran 38:72.

1661 Where are the feet which deserve
to step into the garden of Love?
Where are the eyes which are worthy
of seeing the cypress and jasmine there?
Such feet and eyes are those of a lover consumed by God.
So, show me the one
who deserves to be burned and consumed by Him.

1662 The Beloved asked with a sweet smile,
"How are you? Are you all right?"
Upon seeing such a smile, I answered,
"Now I feel like someone dead
who has just been brought back to life."
I was trying to speak with respect and clarity,
even though the way to Him is scattered and confused.

When I was confused, 1663
caught in grief,
caught in Your Love,
You added yet another chain of trouble.
When I was caught in the curl of Your hair,
You put yet another noose around my neck.

We discovered the cure from Love. 1664
Every moment, we shed our blood for Love.
Love has become our constant friend and companion.
In our every breath, there is the breath of Love.

1665   When Your musk-smelling ropes

became a curtain for the Truth of the Moon,

it kept so many people

from finding their way out of the well of the self.

If Joseph were to see the dimple of Your chin,

he would give up his royalty

and descend to the bottom of the well as a slave.

1666   I want a playful, drunken player

who won't leave the tavern of Your neighborhood,

who is a sultan, whether he is a sultan or not.

God, grant me that drunken player.

I am a slave and servant 1667
of the One who takes me into His soul,
the One who makes my garden and meadow green.
In one moment, He shows me to the world
and makes me famous.
In the next, He changes me into someone like Him
with neither name nor fame.

I am a slave and servant of that Beloved 1668
who is not bored, not hopeless, not weary.
Union is impossible to reach with someone who is weary.
They say, "You are dreaming. You cannot reach Union."
But, nothing reflects on the surface of muddy water.

1669   Name one-by-one all the moon-faced ones,

and maybe by mistake you will mention my Moon.

O people whose eyes cannot see

what is on the other side of the curtain,

look at things through my fiery eyes.

1670   Look for the new. Novelty gives more pleasure.

An old saddle hurts the donkey's back.

O idol, you have also become old.

Where is new beauty?

New sights refresh the heart.

Water never gets weary of fish,   1671
nor do fish ever get weary of water.
The Soul of the Universe never tires of lovers,
nor do lovers ever tire of Him.

The heart which doesn't carry Your Love is an infidel.   1672
It cannot be truly Muslim.
Even if it is prosperous,
a city which is not in awe of Your majesty
should be considered to be merely ruins.

1673   The more my heart tries to satisfy Him,

the more He responds

with a voice like the sharp tip of a sword.

Water drips from His fingertips.

I wonder. Why doesn't He wash His hands in my blood?

1674   Every moment, the Beloved is offering wine

to drunken hearts and souls.

He is making them His full-time company.

The strange thing is that whenever a drop

of His water arrives,

a door opens to an ocean full of pearls.

Every bite you take into your mouth 1675
is transformed into life.
The Sun, Moon and sky keep turning
in order to bring the unseen into existence.

Although words turn around in the mouth, 1676
a wondrous, intense desire
turns around those turning words.
Don't look at the one who turns around his own self.
Look instead, at the One who turns around me.

1677 You don't respect my friendship.
   You pay no attention to my memories.
   You don't even think about Your poor lover.
   Your place is in my eyes.
   From there,
   You scatter pearls into the ocean of my heart
   which is burning with love for You.
   My eyes are full of tears.
   But, You fear neither water nor fire.

1678 The one who ties the untied knot again
   is laughing at himself as well as the world.
   They talk about Union and separation.
   But, one cannot be united until he is separated.

My heart tastes new sweetness every day. 1679
With each new sweetness,
the memory of the old one disappears.
First, my heart ferments the wine of Love,
then serves me.
That makes me lose my mind.

Whenever you are loudly and openly praised, run! 1680
Trouble is hidden behind all that nonsense.
Wherever a heart sings a lullaby,
that house or tavern will soon be ruined.

1681   On a cloudless summer night
when the stars are shining
and the heart of the sky is turning into a rose garden,
there are thousands of signs of Divine Love all around.
Hundreds of sighs rise up from me
which illuminate the mirror of my heart.

1682   A life without seeing friends who are on this path
is either death or a dream.
The water which pollutes you is poison.
The poison which purifies you is pure, clean water.

Too much of anything becomes tiresome and wretched. 1683
Even so, all those things remain
in the house of the Beloved.
Everyone gets tired of things
if they have too much of them.
But, the Beloved never tires
of paying a high price for the soul.

You are such a nice, beautiful companion. 1684
But, be careful.
Don't tip Love's glass,
because the wine could easily spill.
Dust will surely be raised from this dusty world
as long as an insane wind blows.

1685 Let him go. Let him hit his head against a wall.
Let him crack his head and wound his body.
Let blood stain his clothes.
That's when he will return to Me, biting his fingers.
That's when he will remember My words.

1686 I open my arms to You in hope of loyalty.
I bite my fingers during the time of Your cruelty.
But in any case,
I am always thinking about You and asking,
"What is Your order? Tell me.
What do You want me to do?"

When I was wailing and crying out, 1687
He said, "Be quiet."
I became quiet.
Then, He demanded, "I want you to be exuberant."
I became exuberant.
"No," He said. "Calm down."
I calmed down.
Next, He demanded, "I want you to wail and cry."

Night has come. I am in joy. 1688
Tonight, the blessed Beloved is my guest!
My evenings and mornings are different thanks to Love.
I have moved beyond the confines
of the day-and-night cycles of this world.

1689 Don't look at me like I am a stranger.

      I am from this town,

      searching for my house in your quarter.

      I may appear to you as an enemy, but I am not.

      I speak Hindu, but my origin is Turk.[31]

1690 I get the scent of Your breath from the meadows.

      I see the beauty of Your colors in the tulips and jasmine.

      When I am apart from Your gardens,

      I start a conversation.

      My lips mention Your name, and I listen.

---

[31]Metaphorical only.

When I play the ney, it is to cry out for You. 1691
I keep turning around Your neighborhood,
looking for Your scent, Your trace.
You have shown so much kindness,
so much favor to me.
Since I have given You my heart in both worlds,
how could I ask for it back?

Once your candle of love was lit, I became crazy. 1692
I tried restraint,
torturing myself by not looking at you.
But, O beauty, when I did see you,
my eyes went mad with longing.
To see such a peerless beauty turned me simply insane.

1693 We will run until we reach the Beloved.
We will drink until the glass is filled
completely with wine.
Once this clay-kneaded secret passes through,
we will enjoy the dawn of Union.

1694 Since I have come to know the fire and water of Love,
I have been evaporating like water in my heart's fire.
I have given my heart to Love like a rebab,
becoming a friend of Love's plucking and bowing.

Don't suppose that I am free from Your grief   1695
or that I have gotten used to living without You.
I have drunk so much of Your potion of Love
that I will be drunk from one eternity to the last.

As long as I have had any desire,   1696
I have only wanted You from you.
Last night, I set out a table of Love
in honor of my Love for You.
Last night, I had a dream, but I have forgotten it.
All I know is that when I awoke this morning,
I was drunk.

1697   Don't think for even an instant that I see double.

Don't think I have fallen into separation.

Every moment, I receive a new grace.

I know You are my heart and soul.

I know You are my eyes, my head.

I know You are my everything.

1698   Since I have seen Your face,

I have become tired and disgusted with this world.

I used to be a fox,

but I have turned into a lion because of Your light.

O One who, in all of Your greatness,

steps on people's heads,

I bent my neck

and became one of the heads You stepped on.

How long will I turn in the dust and dirt 1699
in exchange for worthless things?
Will I climb the mountain? Will I hide in a cave?
How long will I turn like a child around a doll?
Now is the time for turning around the Beloved!

As long as my soul remains in my body, 1700
I will remain a slave and servant of your coral lips.
Because of your dark, scattered curls,
my heart is unified and at peace.
O ney, wail. Your wailing makes me drunk.
O harp, let your melodies play on. I am your guest.

1701   Since I have come to know Love,

I am no longer bashful.

I have joyfully pulled the curtain away

from the face of the Beloved.

I now play a tune with the Musician of Love.

We have become friends

like the tambourine and the ney.

1702   You may not see straight,

but we are going the right way.

The ones who stray from the road

won't make us get lost.

The one who takes his monthly salary home

will be happy to see us,

because we are like the new Moon.

The closer attention I pay to the things I do, 1703
the more I see
that not using my own eyes is better.
Why should I inconvenience my eyes
when I can see through His?

You know I am far from goodness, 1704
so I am excused if I run away
from well-behaved people.
I am a blind man and He is my cane.
I cannot walk by myself.

1705 I am not afraid of arrows or daggers.

Nor am I afraid

of having my feet tied up or my head cut off.

I am a lover of fire. I drink the fires of hell.

I am certainly not afraid of the gossip of people.

1706 You were timid and quiet. I made you tell stories.

You were a devout ascetic.

I made you a singer of songs.

In this entire Universe, you had no name.

There was no sign of you.

I made you known and made you a teller of signs.

How can we turn down this offer?   1707
We are God's work of art. He is our artist.
We should ascend into His Presence.
There is a table which has been set in the sky
with dishes of gold.
How could we ever be satisfied
with just plain hot water?

I want to pass beyond my soul because of Love for You.   1708
I want to leave both worlds for Your sake.
Please let Your Sun shine through my rain.
I will pass through quickly like a cloud in front of You.

1709 Let's walk around in the moonlight.
Let's go to the rose garden
and watch the sleepless narcissus.
We have skidded across the ice in our ship
for three months.
The time has come, O brothers.
Let's go sail on the water.

1710 We saw that moon-face in the fountain of our heart.
Since that day,
we have kept turning around that fountain.
And, like our heart,
our eyes have kept turning around it, too.

I boil. I am exuberant like blood,   1711
cooking over my own fire.
If that ever makes me wish to forget You,
I pick up the glass
which makes the mind and reason disappear.
You enter into that glass and I drink You.

I have sunk into a whirlpool in the sea of imagination.   1712
No, I am caught by a torrent
which is dragging me to that sea.
O half-sleepy eye, I am a slave and servant
of the One who sees me sleeping even when He sleeps.

1713   Your Love makes knowledge a blunder.
        What is Love? What is knowledge?
        How do we know?
        There is One we should find and know,
        Both worlds are yelling, crying for Him.
        Yet, we don't know anything about Him.
        We don't know Him.

1714   I am Your harp, O Beloved, wailing when You strike.
        But, I am happy that way.
        If You get mad and fight with me,
        I am happy then, too.
        Some feel it is shameful to be scorned
        for being on Love's way.
        I have gladly given up my reputation
        and become friends with such scorn.

They appraised my head, my turban and my robe. 1715
They didn't offer even a penny for all of it.
Haven't you heard my name in the Universe?
I am nothing, nothing, nothing.

I went to the Friends of joy and pleasure last night. 1716
I left the sellers of unripe grapes
and joined the Ones who make sweet grape syrup.
I left the armies of darkness,
choosing instead the moonlight
and sleeping with the Friends
who have awakened from their selves.

1717 I said, "O my ill-tempered Beloved, be kind.
Tell me once more that secret
which You told me before."
He did, and I started to cry.
"Be silent," He said,
"and I will tell it to you again."

1718 That wine which is forbidden to the people
is served freely to the soul of the one
who is free from the body's jail.
Pour us more, O cupbearer.
Never say, "This is the end."
Who knows where our beginning is? Or, our end?

When I heard the word of Love for the first time,   1719
I threw my heart and soul under His feet,
then asked myself if lover and Beloved are two.
They are One. I was seeing double.

I am contented in Absence.   1720
Why do you advise me to return to existence?
On the day I was killed by the sword of Absence,
I was smiling at the ones who were crying for me.

1721   Cupbearer, I am Your drunk tonight.

I have been waiting for You,

longing for wine all day long.

Keep serving me wine.

Save me from the traps of both worlds.

Like every night and day, tonight I am Your prey.

1722   What can I do if the cupbearer offers me red wine?

What can I do if that Beloved,

who is brighter than the Moon, gives me a kiss?

If the glory of Union might come today,

I would be stupid to talk about tomorrow.

I am happy, 1723
because I have been saved from the world's happiness.
I am happy,
because I am drunk without drinking wine.
I don't care about anything else.
I am blessed by this secret happiness.

Night has passed. 1724
We are still with the One who makes us drunk.
Thanks to Your kindness,
we are always doing our work.
We are the lovers of ourselves.
We are our own Beloveds.
We are at the same time
the gathering, the nightingale and the rose garden.

1725   The night says, "I am the friend of the wine drinkers.
I am the soul of the greatly grieved.
And every night, I am an angel of death
to the ones deprived of Love."

1726   A lover walked by and said,
"I am near the world of secrets.
How can I catch and protect a flying bird?"
I answered, "O drunken nightingale,
this meadow has made you drunk."
I repeated this so many times that in the end,
my words got drunk.

Love is an ocean which has no bottom, no boundary.   1727
It is an ocean suspended.
Love is the secret of the One
who has no beginning of the beginning.
All souls are drowned in Love. They live there.
Hope is one drop of that ocean.
The rest of it is fear of separation.

We have looked at each other's faces for a long time now.   1728
Today, too, we look at each other.
Because of the fear of strangers,
we communicate the things in our hearts
through our eyes.
We speak with our eyebrows
and listen with our eyes, too.

1729   I have been annihilated.

Particles of my body have flown to the sky,

the place of my first home.

Every one of them is happy,

drunk and worshiping wine.

Yet, I remain alone in this gloomy dungeon

with faults and shame.

1730   You ordered us

to find our work and do it

before our two arms rested permanently

next to our body.

I reached You and embraced You with joy.

I found my work, because it was ordered by You.

Sometimes, I clap my hands out of happiness. 1731
Sometimes, I bite my fingers because of separation.
Sometimes,
my hands try to catch the Moon in the water.
"Wrong place," the Moon says. "I live in the sky."

If You are a sea, I am a fish in that sea. 1732
If You are a plain, I am a gazelle on that plain.
You breathe through me.
I am a slave and servant of Your breath.
I am Your ney. I am Your ney.

1733   If you are patient,

we will burn away the curtain of your patience.

If you fall asleep,

we will pick the sleep from your eyes.

If you become a mountain,

we will burn you to ashes.

If you become an ocean,

we will drink your water until you are completely dry.

1734   If you like someone, I will make him your enemy.

If you become a thorn, I will hide the rose from you.

If you are a rose, I will throw you into the fire.

Every moment, I will torment you in a different way.

Once I fall into Love, 1735
I will give up my head, my heart, my soul
and both worlds as well.
But, this slave doesn't know
how to live according to Your way.
Tell me Your desire. What do You want?
Whatever it is,
that's what I will do.

If I become arrogant and conceited in my drunkenness, 1736
forgive me.
I am Your drunk.
Don't rush to kill me. I am in Your hands.
You said, "The world I have created is so big, so wide.
Is it still not big enough for you?"[32]
O my soul, you have tied up my feet. Where can I go?

---

[32]Quran 4:97, 29:56, 39:10.

1737 When I see you joyful and happy,

my eyes worship that image.

And like my eyes, my adoring face reflects the same.

When I rub my face in your scattered hair,

I turn around your tall stature like doing Tawaf.[33]

1738 I said, "The envious eyes of the people

give me a headache.

I accept this headache,

because I don't want their eyes to hurt You."

He became an image in my thoughts and said,

"Now, we are out of the sight of those eyes."

---

[33][Arabic] The circumnavigation of the Kaaba.

I said "I should stay separated from Him, 1739
so that that Beloved will become fretful."
I tried hard. I stood patiently firm in my commitment.
But, how could I possibly hide this longing from You?

When I was in silence, when my mouth was closed, 1740
I said many, many things to the ear of your soul.
I do remember everything I said.
I will show you everything tomorrow.

1741   I see a Moon which is beyond new, full and waning.

And, without eyes and sight, I see a way to that Moon.

You said, "Because of that,

the whole world has melted and turned into water."

And oh, what a Moon do I see in that water!

1742   We put on the dress of existence in Absence.

We smiled and passed through existence

as well as Absence.

We untied the ropes one by one

and knocked the tent of patience down from the sky.

I am like a reed pen, writing black on white. 1743
I won't give up, even if they cut off my head,
like they do to the end of that reed.
My head is asking for secrets from me,
but in order to give my head answers,
I will have to give up my head.

I consider friends to be enemies. 1744
I am a foe of every lover, every awakened one.
I am friends with my enemies.
My robe is smeared with blood all the time.

1745   We follow the same creed of Love
as His beautiful, drunken eyes,
that creed which idol-worships His beautiful, curly hair.
Though the Beloved's cruelty breaks hearts,
my heart and soul welcome His breaking.

1746   We would never trade the dirt You stand on
for even a drop of the water of Zamzam.[34]
We would never trade Your grief for joy.
Our shape is the shape of Adam,
but we would never give Adam
even a drop of Your glory.

---

[34] A famous well in the court of the Kaaba which is a miraculously generated source of water from God.

I have died from the troubles of Love! 1747
Come and blow in my face for one moment.
Your breath will make me immortal.
You say, "When we reach Union,
then I will become your close friend."
I said, "What is this? Aren't You ashamed?
Am I not already Your close friend?"

We are God's work of art. 1748
Let us admire the artist.
Why should we stop the desire of the soul?
He sacrifices hundreds of lambs for His slaves.
How can we be satisfied with a glass of hot water?

1749 Don't run away from Me.

       I own you.

       Look at Me.

       I am the light of your face, your eyes.

       Do whatever I do.

       I am the brightness of your affairs.

       Don't ever tire of Me.

       I am your prosperity.

1750 I have become old, but not because of time.

       What has aged me is the endless coyness of the Beloved.

       In every breath,

       I have been cooked, then become raw again.

       At every step, I have been made the bait,

       then the trap again.

O treasure of generosity, 1751
I am the one, not you,
who has sacrificed his head.
Because of that, I am more drunk today than you are.
I will take an oath if you don't believe me.
I want to take an oath,
but why not take wine instead?

That charming Beauty comes drunk every day, 1752
holding in His hand
a glass full of troubles and instigations.
If I drink from that glass,
the bottle of my reasoning will break
and I will lose my mind.
If I don't, He will never let me rest in peace.

1753   Every day in my heart,

I have a joyous, pleasurable Sema.

But, His beauty tells me, "Don't stop there. Go further."

Some people ask, "Why do you eat with five fingers?"

I answer, "Because I have only five fingers, not six."

1754   To us, every particle in the air

is an apple orchard and a rose garden.

Although gold comes from gold mines,

there is a golden spell in every particle

which conceals an ocean.

Though sugar from cane gives sweetness 1755
to the body and soul,
His sugar is different.
When I asked Him,
"Would You give me a piece of Your sugar?"
He answered, "No."
But, His "no" was even sweeter than sugar.

At God's table, when every particle is hungry, 1756
there is endless eating and drink,
yet the table continues to stand.
Despite the need and clamour at that table,
the eating and drinking will never be diminished.
The sustenance at that table will always remain.

1757 Although camels carry sugar,

the one whose eyes are like drunken camels' eyes

is different.

He is even more drunk than his drunken eyes,

so much so that he is not even aware of them.

1758 Every day I receive a new kindness,

a new favor from You.

I keep hearing good news of Your generosity.

I do hope for one more gift from Your ocean-like hands.

It is that hope

which was pledged with fish and bread.

Our Beloved helps lovers through their struggles, 1759
freeing them from oppressive burdens.
Still, He is pleased to hear their cries and wails.
Their souls smile like rose gardens,
while their bodies tremble as if they had malaria.

That Sultan who was the mediator of every sin is gone. 1760
The night which was better than a thousand nights,
that night is gone.
But, even if He were to come back,
He would never find me here.
Tell Him, "He, just like You, was set for the road.
So now, he is gone."

1761   That Beloved whose Beauty cannot be described
came to my home and asked, "How is your heart?"
As He walked in, His robe was dragging.
My heart answered, "Raise the hem of Your robe.
The floors are wet with my bloody tears."

1762   I have died, and no one is weeping for me.
If I come back to life,
I know how I am going to live.
O one who made attempts on my life,
what did you want with me?
I have nothing to do with fools.

On the day of separation, one of my eyes was weeping.   1763
The other one asked, "Why are you weeping?"
On the day of Union, the wet eye said to the dry one,
"Now you can see why you should never stop weeping."

Love is your best and most beautiful friend.   1764
It says to you eloquently,
"Love is not kept from one who wants Love,
especially when one Beauty loves the other."

1765 Because your name is Bahaeddin Veled,[35]

you command souls. You are the Sultan of Eternity.

Don't let the glass of loyalty be broken.

Its pieces may hurt the feet of the drunks.

1766 O Water of Life, whoever tastes Your wine of Love

adds Life to his life.

Death came and smelled me,

but it caught Your scent, and ever since then,

it has left me alone.

---

[35]This rubai is addressed to Rumi's elder son, Sultan Veled, who was named in honor of Rumi's father, Bahaeddin Veled, "Sultânü'l Ûlemâ."

Heads are envious of the ground You step on. 1767
Blind ones are drunk. Deaf ones are confused.
The ones who are annihilated in the sea of cleanliness
are lost gazing at You.

Tonight is not the night to leave the house 1768
and that peerless Beloved
to go to a stranger.
Tonight, all souls must plunge
into the fire of longing and walk like drunks.

1769   Tonight, the cupbearer is serving wine

       not by the glass, but by the pitcher.

       He has plundered hearts and taken away faith.

       He has served so much wine

       that a flood has taken away the house of the mind.

1770   O one who is missing from our Sema,

       there is a Sufi, a learned man,

       and a true sage in our midst.

       If you don't show up, you will become distant.

       Nothing goes away faster than a heart

       whose feet haven't been tied by Love.

Do me a favor. Smile at this slave,   1771
and I will smile back at You in return.
I am weeping bitterly
so my bloody tears can be wine for You,
so my burning heart can be Your kebab.

There are many masters at the tavern of Your sorrow   1772
who are half-sleepy, half-awake, just like Your eyes.
Send this clear, ruby wine to them,
because those lovers are neither drunk with Truth,
nor are they sober.

1773   You are nothing.

But, that nothingness is better than existence.

You are lost in losses,

but your loss is better than gain.

You say, "I have nothing but a handful of dust."

Yet, that dust is envied by the sky.

1774   Once my soul turned its face towards the Essence

and gave up "why's," "what's" and "how's,"

it started seeing eternity.

The secret of Love and the meaning of creation,

concealed for so long,

appeared from behind thousands of curtains.

Unless your soul has been intimate   1775
with this door for a long time,
unless your heart has been filled
with the pain and sorrows of Love
you will never find a road to Us from your self.
You must give up your self
and come to Us through Us.

There is nothing remaining in my ears   1776
except Love's murmur.
There is nothing remaining in my soul,
no reason, no thought,
only the sweetness of Eternity.
The colorless brush of Love has mixed all colors.
Now, not even the remembrance of color remains.

1777   When Your wine is poured into our glass,
the saints who have been concealed in this world
will rise up and appear,
and both the pious and the drunks in the tavern
will run away from us.

1778   My heart-catching Beloved is taking me
to a wonderful place.
He is taking me beyond the realm of body and soul.
At first, I said, "I don't want to go,"
and gave Him all kinds of excuses.
He responded, "Oh, you will go."
And then, He began dragging me away.

There are sorcerers in your eyes to serve you.   1779
They were casting spells to keep me from my sleep.
I said that if I could reach union with you,
I could tie up their hands.
But, you withdrew and they escaped.

On the way of Love, I have seen the smallest details.   1780
On the way of Love,
I have been moved to the front of the line.
Winter has arrived,
and everyone in town is wearing coats of leather and fur.
But now, I don't have even a coat to wear.

1781   Your sweet smile caused me to weep bloody tears.
Your indifference to the world attached me to You.
You now ask, "Where are your oaths and promises?"
I answer, "Your promises and oaths
have made me break them!"

1782   There are dervishes who sit in the presence of God,
who walk on the highest path and are worthy of praise.
If you want their alchemy
to transform the copper of your existence into gold,
meet them. Stay with them.

The hearts of saints are striving for the rank of saint. 1783
The hearts of others are pursuing earthly distractions.
While people are chasing after worldly happiness,
true happiness is seeking the ones
who have an open heart.

Hearts have become restless from the pleasure of Sema. 1784
Like spring clouds, they cannot stay in one place.
O Venus of the Land of Absence,
open the hand of your generosity.
The players of the ney and tambourine
are making useless noise.
They have forgotten Love.

1785   Yesterday, gardens and orchards sent gratitude to You
for saving them from winter.
Your favors and kindness are expressed
on the faces of all the flowers.
The cypress in the meadow has grown taller,
challenging the stature of the others,
and a rose is creating an uproar
with its laughter and fragrance and color.

1786   In order to hide gold from thieves,
they blacken it with soot.
A lover resembles gold.
But, his face never gets blackened-over.
Instead of getting stepped on,
he is passed from one protective hand to another.

They scare drunks with the threat of the muhtesib.[36]   1787
But, everyone knows that your muhtesib gets drunk.
      If the people of this town are good,
    why don't they protect all drunks?

Some people tell stories about the Beyond.   1788
    Some expect help from the Beyond.
Souls keep running out of bodies secretly,
      looking for the Beyond.

---

[36] A supervisor of bazaars and trade in medieval Islamic countries. His duty was to ensure that public business was conducted according to Sharia [religious law].

1789   There are strange birds who hunt only lions.
They have fallen into Your Love
and have no other desires.
Because of You,
the people who live in Your town of Love
live happy, peaceful lives.
It is said that they are upside-down.
Actually, they know neither up nor down.

1790   The ones who are drunk with Your sorrow
are becoming agitated again.
The ones who have become crazy because of You
have started wildly shaking their chains,
tearing apart the robes of patience and reason.

A musician was expecting gifts   1791
for singing with both sorrow and joy.
He considered that his wish could not be ignored.
But, His kindness does not come for free.
It is a pearl, not a pebble.

I am faith. I am faithlessness.   1792
I am clear wine. I am the dregs.
I am old and mature. I am also a young child.
When I die, don't say, "He is dead."
Say, "He was dead, then came to life.
Then, He was taken back by the Beloved."

1793   I am pure. I am clear. I am wine and the dregs of wine.
I am old and mature. I am also a young child.
When I die, don't say, "He is dead."
Say, "He was dead, then came to life.
Then, He was taken back by the Beloved."

1794   I call Him every moment from far away places,
because He is the chapter Joseph
from the almighty Quran.
I said, "My heart became a drop of blood
which flowed out from my eye."
He answered, "No one except you
has ever received such a blessing."

Come and look. 1795
Those are not tears dripping from my eyes,
but drops of blood.
It is my heart which drinks divine wine,
and you can see it coming from my eyes drop by drop.

I was burning insanely for You. Sparks were everywhere. 1796
The joy of being with You
was flowing through my heart like a river.
But, that water was a mirage.
Those sparks were lightning, one strike, then gone.
The story passed. Now only the dream remains.

1797   I swear to God that the image of the face
that has seen Your grace
is glory to my heart as well as to my eyes,
especially if that face sees Your Beauty
throughout eternity.

1798   O Water of Life, whoever tastes Your wine of Love
adds Life to his life.
Death came and smelled me,
but it caught Your scent, and ever since then,
it has left me alone.

That heart-catching Beauty   1799
is closer to me than my soul.
I never call Him,
because the one who is called
is the one who is not here.

O heart, no harm will come to you from death.   1800
How can you become lifeless once you become pure soul?
First, you came from the sky to the Earth.
In the end, you will ascend back to the sky.

1801 We are drunk because of a heart-catching charmer.

But, that beloved is running away from us.

He is pure, clear reason.

Reason most certainly runs away from drunks.

1802 Because of Your power,

neither friend nor enemy remains.

At Your assembly, neither cup nor wine remain.

O Beloved, I know You drank my blood,

because the scent of it on Your sweet lips still remains!

This night is passing by so beautifully, 1803
but no one can understand its charm and beauty.
Sleep is astonished by the beauty
of the rose and jasmine gardens
where souls are strolling
and lovers are enchanted just by looking at each other.

Something is turning around in my head tonight. 1804
My heart has become a bird, circling in the air.
Every particle of my body is turning separately.
I wonder. Is the Beloved turning around devotion?

1805   A good rider deserves a black horse for night riding.

   A good cauldron deserves a good skimmer.

   But, when a bad one becomes a bride,

   no dowry or sweetmeats are needed.

1806   Your sharp, sensible mind kills wise ones.

   First, it makes them cry. Then, it kills them.

   The sultans of our time put their enemies on the gallows,

   but in Your dominion, they are killed without gallows.

That sugar-mine heart, that bale of sugar did not come.   1807
That Water of Life with its oceans of pearls did not come.
I said to myself, "I should go
and talk with Him nicely
to win His heart."
But, when I saw Him, no words came!

Favors from the Beloved's compassion   1808
come to the lover who endures Love's suffering.
The Beloved said,
"In your short life, search for Union with Me.
Union is the only answer to your screams."

1809   I was happy and cheerful, filled with Your Love.
When You left, my joy and happiness left, too.
But, You filled me up so much with Your Love
that now not even its memory can reach me.
Now, cause and effect are hot air to me.
How can one build a mud house on the sea?

1810   The sleepy head is the one who doesn't know Him.
The one who knows Him could never sleep!
Every night, Love whispers to me, looking into my eyes,
"Pitied is the one who is asleep, who is without Him."

When fate gives knowledge and wisdom to someone, 1811
it cuts his sustenance and throws him into poverty.
It fills the ignorant one with wealth instead of wisdom
and turns him into a storehouse or granary.

That Love which was lightning and glory 1812
scattered all of my belongings.
Not even a patched cloak was left for me.
The stream of Love
which had been barely reaching the hem of my robe
became a torrent rising all the way up to my neck.

1813   That cypress-like Beauty is my soul.

        My body was ashamed when He arrived.

        He came as He was

        and has changed me into the way I am now.

1814   When pearls are scattered from the sky,

        every particle wants to ascend to the place of its origin.

        But, because of the selfishness of the wind,

        they are being blown away from the Sun.

How can I resist the scent of Your shirt   1815
when it makes even the sky tear up its veils?
Where is the sweet-smelling shirt
of that beautiful Joseph?
If it reappears today,
it will take on the same scent as Yours.

There is a mind-catching Beloved   1816
who is known to subjugate mountains.
I said to Him,
"You untied and scattered Your hair."
He said, "So many heads keep losing themselves
in the tips of those hairs!"

1817 After seeing You, how could anyone not be astonished?

If his face doesn't smile,

if his mouth doesn't open wide,

if he doesn't laugh ecstatically with joy,

then he must be like a stone,

good only for a dungeon wall.

1818 O ney player, your ney is as sweet as sugarcane.

If you do not come, our Khosrow[37]

cannot join with his Shirin.

When you play to the Universe in early dawn,

this old world becomes young again.

---

[37]A love story about the Persian Shah Khosrow Parwix II (591-628 CE) and the Armenian Princess Shirin.

If you cultivate only thorns,   1819
you will scratch the face of the rose.
If you want it to produce colorful blooms,
you need to cultivate that rose.
Barley grains are seeds. This world is like a mill.
If you take bricks to the mill,
you will bring back only dust.

If you want immortality,   1820
look for the sign and trace of Absence.
Walk straight on the path of Absence
until it disappears.
Keep going until you reach benevolence.
Advance bravely, so that you may see immortal life.

1821   Once I step onto the desert of Nothingness,

an uproar will be heard

from the invisible Land of Absence.

In astonishment Absence will say,

"I haven't seen anyone in either world

as Love-crazy as he is."

1822   You are my soul, my only Beloved in both worlds.

You are my helper

and the answer to all my troubles and sorrows.

For me, there is no one but You in either world.

You offer me kindness and forgive my sin.

I never thought you could evict me from your heart,   1823
could pack up my belongings
and throw me out into the mud.
I praised you a great deal
to both my friends and enemies.
What a pity you could dismiss me with such shame!

When there is harmony,   1824
when your heart is contented with Love,
you see new things
and find new meanings in every beauty.
If one tooth outgrows itself,
grows much longer than the other thirty-one teeth,
your body might as well be toothless.

1825   Your heart has the disposition of a Zoroastrian.[38]
Although you don't eat straw like a donkey,
you carry straw on your back.
If a mirror shows your ugliness,
you get mad and, with one blow of your fist,
you shatter that mirror.

1826   I have shed bloody tears because of Your Love.
The soul in my body has wailed because of Your sorrow.
O Soul of the world,
You are not even aware of my situation.
Fate has used You as an excuse to crush me.

---

[38]Contrary to the Muslim belief in the existence of the one God, the Zoroastrians believed in the existence of two, one God of good and one God of evil.

You are the sultan of words, yet you keep silent. 1827
You are the messenger of the tongue,
yet you don't act like a messenger.
O sun, why are you hiding in the mud?
It is breaking the heart of the sky.

Joy, joy, O my friends, joy! 1828
Thousands of words of freedom
are coming from that Moon
who has freed Himself from the bondage of the Earth.
He says, "I have been kind to lovers.
I have granted their wishes."
Yes, O Moon. You have given.
You have given,
You have given!

1829 O insignificant one, the night has passed,
and your heart has yet to be satisfied.
If that Moon doesn't touch your hand,
you will remain insignificant.
All your friends have fallen asleep.
The only thing left for you to do
is to drink ruby wine and stay awake.

1830 The Earth has become green,
adorned by gardens and meadows everywhere.
Everything is smiling,
reflecting that immortal Beauty.
There are rubies on every corner
which have come from the Divine Mine.
There are souls everywhere
which have reached that Soul.

You don't pay attention to my sorrows,   1831
much less take them seriously.
You said, "I am yours. Why are you worrying?"
I said, "You may go,
and I will keep burning down like a candle.
That is why I am worrying."

Sometimes I fall into the fire of separation   1832
which darkens my world.
Sometimes, I am taken by the pleasures
which brighten my soul.
Unfortunately, the occurrences of both of them
have been indelibly written on my forehead
by fate and time.

1833   You are the heretic, the heresy,

        even worse than that.

        You are also faith.

        And, You are the source of both of them.

1834   If I weren't worried about people's envy,

        I would do the thing I mentioned last night.

        Even if that envy didn't exist,

        I would still stay confused,

        drunk and exuberant all the time.

If the force of longing for the Beloved   1835
was not so strong in me,
how could this beggar be in the company of a Sultan?
If His ancient, infinite kindness did not exist,
the Joseph of the soul
would never have been displayed
and sold in the market.

There aren't any signs of hope in Love's desert.   1836
But sometimes, new hope comes out of desperation.
O heart, don't give up.
Even a willow tree grows dates in the garden of the soul.

1837 I am not beautiful, but I worship Beauty.
It am not wine, but I am drunk with wine.
I am not a man of prayers. That is true.
But, I am a drunk of Your tavern.

1838 O hajji,[39] if you think I am a drunk
who is going the wrong way, stay sober.
Become a wise man
and boast with your prayers and piety.
But, you should know this very well:
Your conceited way
does not lead to the bridge you expect.

---

[39][Arabic] Honorific title for Muslim person who has successfully completed the Hajj [pilgrimage] to Mecca.

If you are looking for the soul's mansion, 1839
you are soul.
If you are looking for a bit of bread,
you are bread.
If you understand this subtle point,
then you already know the secret:
Whatever you are looking for, that is what you are.

When you choose to, you jump like a gazelle. 1840
When you strike, you are as hard as iron.
O clever bird,
you are joyously clinging with your two feet
on the same rose branch as we are.

1841   If Your secrets could be shared,

        the Earth and sky would be turned into rose gardens.

        If arrogance weren't everywhere in the world,

        every pharaoh would become Moses, son of Imran.

1842   Wouldn't it be nice

        if you were fair and treated me justly?

        Or, if you were to remember this poor one more often?

        You told me, "I do remember you often."

        Yes, I have heard that.

        But, I know the way you remember things.

If you knew the secrets of Love, 1843
you would give your life for this way.
As long as you stay your own drunk, you are restless.
When you become His drunk,
you wake up immediately.

If there is One who burns your heart, 1844
if your heart is filled with the desires of Love,
you should know that this sweet burning
is your happiness.
Your wailing and crying
is your relief,
your divine help.
Make this wailing a friend of your every breath.

1845   Even though You don't greet me in return,

You are still full of joy, like wine,

which acts as a greeting.

You are the shepherd of the whole world,

the soundness of all souls.

You repel the wolves,

even though You don't make a sound.

1846   You said, "You are insane."

I said, "You are the one who is insane,

because you are looking for reason from Love."

You said, "You are shameless. Your face is like iron."

"Yes," I said.

"What else could you expect from a mirror?"[40]

---

[40]In medieval Asia Minor, mirrors were made of polished metal.

I said to the doctor,   1847
"I have a deep pain. Can you prescribe me a remedy?"
That doctor pretended to know something,
held my wrist for a pulse and asked,
"Where is your pain?"
I took his hand
and put it over my broken, impassioned heart.

I asked, "Why are You making a sour face?   1848
You aren't vinegar."
"Because," He said,
"you mix with the enemy like wine and water."
I answered, "Next time with the enemy,
I will be like oil and water."
He laughed, then said, "Go away. In saying and doing,
you are always switching
from one thing to its opposite."

1849   I asked my heart, "To be on the road to Love,
what is required of the self?"
My heart answered, "For the self,
the road to Love is humiliation."
I asked, "Then, why are you, O heart,
afraid of humiliation?"
My heart answered, "Your self's pride
shuts Love's door in your face!"

1850   You think that your Beloved
is unaware of your sorrow.
The Beloved has not changed.
He is in the house.
Yet, you are not aware of Him.
Are you aware that you assume He is unaware?

You came from your origin smiling like a rose. 1851
You are cheerful,
because you are aware
of your good fortune, your good fate.
You are as fresh as spring flowers and free like a cypress,
yet not at all bound by this Earth.

The Moon came into His presence saying, 1852
"You are my soul."
The Moon, prideful before the crowd,
was hoping He would say, "You are mine."
But, He replied,
"You are one of My least worthy slaves."

1853   We are being carried away by our desire

to see the face of that Sultan.

We are submerged like fish in His Love,

His sea of eternal life.

Dawn has broken. Morning has come.

We are upset by these uproars, this untimely morning.

We are begging for redress from this untimely noise.

1854   Are you aware of your self?

Are your mind and perspective confused?

Or, have you turned into a mind and a perspective?

The house of the heart

is full of beautiful countenances.

Yet, you are sitting in the corner, glimpsing furtively.

How long will You keep burning my harvest? 1855
How long will You stay away from me
while I am burning?
How long will You help my enemies?
I am engulfed in Your sorrow.
How long will You ignore me?

O my beauty, I am the lover and you are the beloved. 1856
You shouldn't be hurt by any of my words.
Either give my heart back to me
or accept with love everything I do.

1857 I am not Me.

   If I were to become Me for even a moment,

   I would crush this world to pieces.

   If I were to merge with the One who took my heart,

   if I were to become Him,

   like a tree, I would uproot Myself from this world.

1858 God is telling you, "O restless one, give up people.

   You are Mine, My special one.

   Get used to Me, because in the end,

   I will be the One who comes to you

   in your night of solitude."

I said, "Know, but don't tell. 1859
That way, your name will stay clean.
The beauty of a person consists of his solicitude,
his discretion, and his refraining from gossip."
He asked, "But, how can one keep a secret?
There is a Sultan here
who splits one piece of hair into forty pieces
with His gaze."

You said, "You humiliated me in front of them." 1860
"You destroyed my honor. You made me helpless."
Then, you started to cry.
I said, "Stay in the back.
You went up to the front and walked the wrong way.
Look and see what a bad position you have put me in."

1861   I am not me. You are not you. And, you are not me.

But, I am me, you are you and you are me.

O beauty of Hotan,[41] I am so confused about you that I am not sure:

Am I you or are you me?

1862   Every day, thanks to Your Love,

You send a new shirt to Your lover.

O Joseph of our time, I am Your Jacob.

Your shirt heals the blind.

It keeps opening my eyes ever wider.

---

[41]A city in Western China famous for the beauty of its inhabitants.

You will not speak a single word   1863
worthy of your character,
nor will you be happy for even a moment
until you cut the neck of sorrow.
If you don't let go of worries,
you won't be able to escape sadness.
One can't have a conversation
with someone who makes them weary.
This is clear.

O moon-faced Beloved,   1864
You call me into Your presence every moment.
You ask about my situation,
even though You know it very well.
You are a walking cypress. Words are like wind for You.
When I talk, You sway and nod Your head.

1865   Your inclination is never to put away the table.
You love eating so much
that you want to keep the table full all the time.
Where is your inclination
to uplift your desire and your love?
Although you say, "Thanks to God,"
you do not say, "In the name of God,
the most merciful, the most compassionate."[42]
You want dinner before it is even dawn.

1866   A drunk neighbor gives you more drunkenness.
When you become drunk,
you will free yourself from existence.
If you sit in the gathering with God's men,
take only wine.
Forget about food, fire and water.

---

[42]The phrase recited before each sura [chapter] of the Quran.

A kiss from His ruby-colored lips   1867

has filled the world with the smell of apples and pears.

He has torn apart the curtains of both day and night

out of Love for His own beautiful face.

What a face it is!

Members of different nations argue that Rumi belongs to their country, which is understandable. They are all right to some extent. In spite of this patriotic fervor, most everyone accepts that the treasure of Rumi cannot fit in any one country's boundaries. He was certainly much larger than life. At the same time, though, he was very close to mankind, without religious or racial boundaries. Mevlânâ is like an infinitely large umbrella covering all we have and beyond.

-Nevit O. Ergin

Appendices

Ishq

"Among classical Muslim authors, the notion of love (*Ishq*) was developed along three conceptual lines: natural love, intellectual love and divine love. [. . .] The term *ishq* is used extensively in Sufi poetry and literature to describe a 'selfless and burning love for Allah.' It is the core concept in the doctrine of Islamic mysticim as is key to the connection between man and God [. . .] In most languages, it literally means 'love.' [. . .] Despite the linguistic, cultural or technical meanings, Sufis believe that *ishq* can only be associated to the Divine." (Wikepedia)

We have included the word Ishq at the bottom of each page of quatrains in this fourth volume of *The Rubáiyát of Rumi, The Ergin Translations* to honor Rumi and his tradition.

Notes on These Translations

Since the first English translation of forty-eight poems from Rumi's *Dîvân-i Kebîr* was published by R.A. Nicholson in 1898, Rumi has slowly, but surely become more and more well-known to the Western world. In particular, the first 24 years of our 21st century have seen an explosion of commentaries, research projects, and collections of Rumi's poetry. Rumi is shared through books, in sermons at places of worship, at colleges and universities and through social media.

So why these translations by Ergin? Just as there could never be too many new performances of Beethoven, there can never be too many collections of Rumi. Each brings a slightly different perspective to the world, and each perspective speaks in a voice which reaches the ones who need to hear it. And Rumi needs to be heard by everyone in this world, especially in times as tumultuous as these. He is recognized by many as the greatest and most prolific mystic poet of all time. We regard his poetry as sacred texts.

Nevit Ergin, Translator

Nevit Ergin (1928-2015) had been introduced to Rumi in 1956 by Hasan Lutfi Shushud (1902-1988), author of *Masters of Wisdom of Central Asia* and *Fakir Sözleri* and a Master of the Itlak Yolu Sufi Path of Annihilation and Absolute Liberation.

Ergin was looking for something which went beyond the lectures, books, philosophy courses, religion and everything else he had tried up to that point in his life. On one auspicious Sunday, he had occasion to meet Mr. Shushud. That day was the beginning of a lifelong friendship.

On one of his first visits, Ergin took with him a book of selected Rumi poems entitled *Gül Deste* [*Bouquet of Roses*] just published by the Turkish scholar, Abdülbakî Gölpinarli (1900-1982). When Ergin asked Mr. Shushud about the value of the book, Mr. Shushud went out into his garden, cut a long-stemmed rose, returned and gave it to him. Ergin pressed the rose between the pages of that book which he would carry with him for the rest of his life. Mr. Shushud proceeded to tell him that he would need to experience lots of hunger, lots of a type of breath work, and lots of mental suffering. Reading, discussing and fellowship would come later. He added, "If you choose one book, the *Dîvân-i Kebîr of Mevlânâ Celâleddîn Rumi* will do it."

It was not until the late 1980's that Ergin began "to know Mevlânâ." Although he was living in the United States, he continued to travel several times a year to Turkey. He first translated into English selections of Gölpinarli's Turkish translations of the *Dîvân-i Kebîr*, specifically, selections of the *Rubáiyát*. These were published by Hohm Press under the title, *Crazy as We Are*. The following year, 1993, Larson Publications published *Magnificent One*, a selection of ghazals [longer lyric poems, or odes] from the *Dîvân*. Ergin was encouraged by that publisher to translate what he thought was the entirety of the ghazals from Gölpinarli's Turkish translations. He accomplished the translations of those ghazals between 1992 and 2003, and they were published as the *Dîvân-i Kebîr of Mevlânâ Celâleddîn Rumi* (in 22 volumes) through his own publishing company, Echo Publications, and the Ministry of Culture of the Republic of Turkey. It was also in 1992 that he formed the non-profit organization, the Society for Understanding Mevlânâ.

Our Friendship

Hasan Shushud was also the one who introduced me to Rumi. When I stayed with him for a few weeks in 1972,[1] we visited a small building where he pointed out some large, ornate double doors, and said, "These are the doors to the house of Mevlânâ. One day you must get to know him."

The day before I left Istanbul, Nevit Ergin visited Mr. Shushud, Mr. Shushud introduced us, and that was for me the beginning. I went to work for Ergin in Michigan in

---

[1] There is a more detailed account of my time with Mr. Shushud in Ergin's *The Sufi Path of Annihilation*, published by Inner Traditions in 2014.

his nursery school, and although I stayed as his employee for only three years, we stayed friends until his death in 2015.

When he began translating Rumi, I helped him connect with publishers for his first two collections. With the first volume of the *Dîvân-i Kebîr* project in 1993, I was responsible for book design, printing and typesetting. I was also put on the board of the newly formed Society for Understanding Mevlânâ as a consultant, but my role was limited to working on the books.

Ergin was a plastic surgeon. Over the years, I visited him fairly frequently in his office. After the late 1980s, whenever he was between patients, he would invariably be translating a ghazal. He would read whatever he was translating to me, always excited, and me always nodding my head in agreement, but not understanding his excitement. It took another ten years for me to see why he so often said to me, "The *Dîvân* is like a mine field. You never know when it will blow your heart and mind."

Ergin moved back to live in Turkey from 1996 through 1999, and we did not reconnect on a regular basis until after I retired in 2012. During the interim, he published *Tales of a Modern Sufi*, as well as, with Will Johnson, *Insane with Love* and *Forbidden Rumi*. But, from 2012 until 2015, I spent one week a month helping him get his final works completed. During those three years, he completed a number of new short stories (as yet unpublished), *The Sufi Path of Annihilation*, a retranslation of *Volume 9* of the *Dîvân-i Kebîr*, *Unknown Rumi*, and *Mevlânâ Rubâîler* with Merâle Ekmekçioğlu. (See below)

The *Replica*

Over the years of traveling between the United States and Turkey, Ergin became good friends with Erdoğan Erol, the Director of the Mevlânâ Museum in Konya, Turkey. Thanks to Erol's support, the museum gave him permission to photograph some of the artwork of the *Dîvân-i Kebîr* housed in the museum (numbers 68 and 69), and in 1993, replications of those photos were printed in the first volume of Ergin's translations of the *Dîvân's* ghazals.

Then, in 2006, the Turkish Ministry of Culture and the Mevlânâ Museum gave Ergin permission to commission the production of a microfiche of the entire hand-written, two-volume set of that *Dîvân*; to take color photographs of all of its artwork; and, most important, to reproduce one thousand copies of the set. We refer to this set as the *Replica*. Thanks to the financial backing of Edmond Gorginian, the publication was made a reality in 2007 through Echo Publications and the Society for Understanding Mevlânâ.

Ergin's desire was to make it possible for more people to read the *Dîvân* in its original, hand-written Farsi and for more people to be able to translate from the original Farsi directly into English. He set out to get the *Replica* placed in libraries and universities across the United States and Europe and to make it available to purchase on the internet.

And, of course, once Ergin had the *Replica* in his hands, thanks to the help of those who could read the original text, he was able to confirm his own translations.

Ergin's *Mevlânâ Rubâîler*

Ergin was profoundly aware of the criticism that his English translations were from the Turkish and not directly from the original Farsi. As a result, as he translated the *Rubáiyát* from Gölpinarli's Turkish, he consulted with scholars from Stanford University who were able to read the *Replica* text. But, he also was determined to publish a book with a photograph of each rubai in its hand-written original Farsi, accompanied by a Turkish translation, and an English translation as well. He believed this would encourage others to explore each of Rumi's quatrains on their own.

Ergin worked on the English translations himself from 2007 until just before his passing in 2015, and during that same period, worked on the Turkish translations with Merâl

Ekmekçioğlu, who had *Mevlânâ Rubâîler* published in 2016 through Sarayönü Gazete–Matbaa in Konya, Turkey.

The Rubáiyát of Rumi, The Ergin Translations

Unlike *Mevlânâ Rubâîler*, our four-volume set is an English-only version. Our goal was to provide a more affordable version, and one which could be easily picked up to read in any place, at any time.

We chose to publish Ergin's translations of the *Rubáiyát of Rumi* for several reasons. Although selections of his translations have been published before, this is the first time his translations of all 1,867 quatrains will have been published - in English only - in their entirety. But we also chose to publish these quatrains because they are short, yet remarkably powerful. In some of them, an idea can hit you square in the eye and rattle your whole perception of life. Some may speak to you superficially and others at the deepest of levels.

In finalizing the translations for publication, I was able to collaborate with my dear friend, Shahzad Mazhar, who has studied Middle Eastern poetry, who is able to read the original medieval Farsi texts of the *Dîvân-i Kebîr Replica*, and who loves Rumi's poetry.

Clearly, Ergin's work is not a word-by-word translation, and he made no effort to adhere to the quatrain format. However, the remarkable spiritual work which he accomplished in his lifetime allowed him to capture more deeply the essence of Rumi's poetry. That said, since English was Ergin's second language (after Turkish), others have questioned the authenticity of some of his word choices. Thanks to Shahzad, I was able to confirm that every one of Ergin's translated quatrains was matched in its essence to the *Replica* text.

Of note is that the more earthly quatrains needed more of our attention to the English than those reflecting the concepts of Absence or reflecting Absence itself.

Also of note is the translation of Rubai 809 in Volume 2. In a bow to Hasan Shushud, Ergin added footnotes to show the concordance of the language used in Shushud's *Masters of Wisdom of Central Asia*:

> All forms and shapes are from base matter.*
> The Divine† is the One who forms them.
> The world of Essence‡
> doesn't come to the world of appearances,**
> but it manifests in the world of appearances.

*Hasan Shushud, *Masters of Wisdom of Central Asia* (Rochester, VT: Inner Traditions, 2014), 167. Heyâlâ [matter].
†Shushud, *Masters*, 172. Lâhût [divinity].
‡Shushud, *Masters*, 158. Ayn [essence].
**Shushud, *Masters*, 172. Nâsût [humanity].

And finally of note, in books and articles and online, the spellings of names differ wildly according to language and religious tradition. For example, for the Rumi biographer Ahmet Eflâkî, his first name is seen as Ahmet, Ahmed and Ahmad, and Eflâkî is seen as Eflaki and Aflaki. If any verbiage is quoted in our four volumes, the source spellings were used with no effort made to reach consistency or "correct" English spelling.

Rumi recited his verses in couplets. The rubai is the shortest form he used, each rubai being two couplets, or a quatrain. In fact, rubai is the Arabic word for quatrain. Each rubai expresses a complete, epigrammatic idea. The first, second and fourth lines rhyme, while the third line is usually free.

This form has been known in classic Islamic literature since the 10th century. However, it was an unknown form in the Western world until the late 1850's when the English poet Edward Fitzgerald (1809-1883) published his translation of the *Rubaiyat of Omar Khayyam* (1048-1131).

The first *Rubaiyat of Rumi*, selections translated into English by A.J. Arberry (1905-1973) appeared in 1949 under the title, *Mystical Poems of Rumi 1, First Selection, Poems 1-200*.[2]

Our current publication of *The Rubáiyát of Rumi, The Ergin Translations*, includes all of Rumi's quatrains found in the Osman al-Mavlavi compilation, described below.

There are 1,867 quatrains total in our four volumes, although 52 of the quatrains are duplicates. Considering the immense amount of material that had to be hand-copied for the Dîvân, it is no wonder there are so many duplicates. We have included each one as it appears in the *Replica*, making a note in our concordance where each set of duplicates can be found.

The Works of Rumi

Rumi created numerous works, all with the same messaging, but delivered in different forms. They include the *Dîvân-i Kebîr* (two volumes of poetry in various meters and forms including the ghazal, terci-bend, murabbe and rubai), the *Mesnevî* (six volumes of poetry all in one meter), *Mektubat* (letters), *Mecâlis-i Seb'a* (seven sermons) and *Fîhi Mâ Fîhi* (conversations).

For many years, Rumi's work most well-known to the West was the *Mesnevî*, a collection of stories and anecdotes written in AA, BB, CC couplets. He dictated this great work to his last close companion, Çelebi Hüsameddin (1225-1284), beginning in 1258 and continuing until his death in 1273. It is the most interpreted work in the Islamic world after the Quran and the Hadith.[3]

His second most well-known work is his *Dîvân-i Kebîr* (also known as *Dîvân-i Shems-i Tebriz*). *Dîvân-i Kebîr* means "big notebook," dîvân being the name given to the notebook in which writers collect their poems. Rumi's reputation among so many audiences as the greatest mystic love poet of all time is thanks in part to the work found in his *Dîvân*.

---

[2] Nevit O. Ergin, *Private Notes*.
[3] Erdoğan Erol, *Mevlânâ's Life, Works and the Mevlânâ Museum* (Konya: Altunari Ofset Ltd. Şti, 2005),27-36.

The Origins of the *Dîvân-i Kebîr*

As mentioned before, after he met the Sufi mystic, Shams of Tabriz, Rumi began reciting poems for his *Dîvân*. We do not know of any one poem which Rumi actually wrote down. He recited his poems extemporaneously, responding to various questions and events or reflecting on his own mystical experiences. His words were written down by scribes known as Kâtib-i Esrar (Secretaries of Secrets).

Unfortunately, Rumi's *Dîvân* was not compiled during his lifetime. However, in the next century, a number of compilations of the notes of these scribes were created.

The Hasan ibni Osman-al Mavlavi Compilation

We used only the one compilation which Ergin had photographed and eventually published as the *Replica*. It is a two-volume compilation, currently housed in the Mevlânâ Museum in Konya, Turkey as numbers 68 and 69. It was compiled by Hasan ibni Osman-al Mavlavi between July 2, 1367 and October 13, 1368. It is in two large volumes, measuring 17 inches tall and 12½ inches wide, containing a total of 326 pages. The work is in Farsi, the language of poetry of Rumi's time, with some words scattered throughout in Arabic, Turkish, and even Greek. The total number of individual verses exceeds 44,000, and they are formed into rubáiyát, ghazals, terci-bends and murabbes.

As we have previously mentioned, there are 1,867 rubáiyát, or quatrains, in the Osman-al Mavlavi compilation.

The compilation has 3,327 ghazals. The ghazal is a longer form of lyric love poetry dating back to 7th century Arabic poetry. Its theme is often that of the pain of separation. Each verse is a couplet of the same poetic meter, with a rhyme scheme of AA, BA, CA, DA and so on. The couplets of each ghazal fit under the umbrella of one theme, but each couplet is independent in meaning, and the connection to the other couplets is sometimes obscure. The final couplet includes the author's pen name. In Rumi's *Dîvân*, Rumi often ends with the mention of Shams of Tabriz, thereby attributing authorship to him.

The compilation has 37 terci-bends. The terci-bend form is a didactic poem. It has the same stylistic features of the ghazal, but each couplet is followed by a couplet with its own separate rhyme scheme. The terci-bend is a much longer form, and the couplets are divided into stanzas of five to ten couplets each. One couplet is repeated at the end of each stanza and each stanza "bends back" to express the theme of the first section in a different way.

The compilation has six murabbes. The murabbe form developed out of the quatrain form. It is actually a series of quatrains, each one tied thematically. Each verse features the same final line.

This compilation was first translated from Farsi into Turkish by the Turkish scholar Abdülbakî Gölpinarli. He published the first volume of his seven volume *Dîvân-i Kebîr Mevlânâ Celâleddîn* in 1957 and the final one in 1974.

For his *Dîvân-i Kebîr Mevlânâ Celâleddîn*, Gölpinarli also referenced three other sources: (1) the *Dîvân* registered at the Library of the University of Istanbul, No. 334, which was compiled in the 15th century; (2) the *Dîvân* owned by Gölpinarli himself, prepared in 1691 in Baghdad; and (3) the eight volumes of the *Kulliyât-e shams yâdîwân-é kebîr -e mawlânâ jalâluddîn* prepared by Persian scholar Badî'uzzamân Forûzânfar (1904-1979) which were completed in 1965. However, Gölpinarli considered the Osman-al Mavlavi compilation his most reliable source.[4]

Other Contributors
to the West's Knowledge of Rumi

In the 1950's, Gölpinarli and Forûzânfar were the two scholars most responsible for increasing the Western world's interest and knowledge of Rumi. Ergin knew both of them.

---

[4] Mevlânâ Celâleddîn Rumi Nevit O. Ergin, Translator, Divan-i Kebir, Meter 1 (Walla Walla, WA: Turkish Republic Ministry of Culture & Current, 1995), vii; Ergin, Private Notes, 2015.

Gölpinarli was from a family with a Mevlevi tradition. His Farsi and Arabic were strong and his life was devoted to the study of Rumi. He translated into Turkish not only the *Dîvân-i Kebîr*, but all of the rest of Rumi's works as well. The last part of his life was spent at the Mevlânâ Museum in Konya cataloging all of their works related to Rumi.

Forûzânfar was a renowned modern scholar of Persian literature, which consists mostly of poetry, and was considered the Persian authority on Rumi. He produced considerable critical works and commentaries on Rumi in Persian which made it easier for Western scholars to translate Rumi. Most importantly, he researched various compilations to determine the full scope of Rumi's poetry and included all of Rumi's ghazals, terci-bends, and rubáiyát in a single work of eight volumes entitled, the *Kulliyât-e shams*, mentioned above. As part of his research, he determined which verses were Rumi's and which were created by others, but mistakenly attributed to Rumi.

We would be remiss not to mention some of the other scholars who gave the West its introductions to Rumi, contributing a foundation for further study. These include but are not limited to E.H. Whinfield (1836-1922), Reynold A. Nicholson (1868-1945), A.J. Arberry (1905-1973), Annemarie Schimmel (1922-2003), and the Turkish scholar Şefik Can (1909-2005). The American poet and professor Coleman Barks (1937-) has provided Americanized versions of Rumi. Barks is perhaps the most responsible for making Rumi the most popular poet in North America today.

And, as we mentioned at the opening of these notes, in the first 24 years of our 21st century, there has been an explosion of commentaries, research projects, and collections of Rumi's poetry by contributors too numerous to name. Such an explosion may be saying that if we haven't taken Rumi very seriously before, now is the time to do so.

And, we look forward to the future as others continue to contribute to our knowledge of this greatest of mystic poets.

The Importance of Islam in Rumi's Life

Rumi was raised a Muslim in Balkh, (present-day Afghanistan), his family eventually settling in Konya, Turkey, in 1228 at the request of the Seljuk ruler Keyqubâd I. At that time, Rumi was 21 years old. His father, Muhammed Bahaeddin Veled, was the Sultânü'l Ûlemâ [Sultan of the Scholars], and once in Konya, he assumed responsibilities of heading a medresse [theological school] there. When his father passed in 1231, Rumi became his successor, taking on all of his father's duties, students and disciples.

By then, Rumi was already a scholar of many disciplines, an expert on Sharia [Islamic religious law], the Quran, and the Hadith [sayings and traditions of the Prophet Muhammad].[5] Even after he met Shams of Tabriz, he stated:

> As long as my soul stays in my body,
>
> I am a slave of the Quran
>
> and the dust on the path of Muhammad.
>
> If anyone interprets my words
>
> differently than this,
>
> I will break with him and reject his words.
>
>   -Rubai 735 (Volume 2)

Naturally, we would expect Rumi's poetry to reflect his Islamic Tradition. However, Rumi's message is universal. His Islamic roots do not change his appeal for those of all religious backgrounds, nor does it diminish the existence of other messengers of God from other religious traditions and the truth of their messages. As he clearly states:

> I came here to unify,
>
> not to divide.[6]

---

[5]Erol, *Mevlânâ's Life*, 12-13.
[6]Erol, *Mevlânâ's Life*, 7.

As he also clearly states:

> There is neither question nor answer
> on the way to Love,
> but only a mystery.
> The lover never answers to any human orders.
> This is a matter of Absence, not existence.
>
> -Rubai 1314 (Volume 3)

Islamic and Sufi Terms Commonly Used in Rumi's Poetry

Eid [Arabic] A religious holiday celebrating the end of Ramadan.

Kaaba [Arabic "the cube"] An ancient stone structure built as a house of monotheistic worship. Located inside the Grand Mosque (the most sacred Al-Masjid al Harām) in Mecca. Considered to be the center of the Muslim world and a unifying focal point for Islamic worship.

Qibla [Arabic] The direction Muslims face to pray, fixed as the direction of the Kaaba.

Ramadan [Arabic] The ninth month of the Islamic calendar, observed by Muslims worldwide as a month of fasting, prayer, reflection and community.

Sema [Turkish] A Sufi ceremony performed as a remembrance of God. In the Mevlevi Order, which was established after the death of Mevlânâ Celâleddîn Rumi by his son, Sultan Veled, the performers are known as Whirling Dervishes.

The Role of Music in Rumi's Life

Rumi introduced "turning" accompanied by music to his disciples in a ceremony known as Sema. During the ceremony, participants allowed the music and their turning to carry them into an ecstatic state. Because of the practice, after Rumi's passing and with the formal organization of the Mevlevi Order of Sufism by Rumi's son, Sultan Veled, members of the order were and still are known as the Whirling Dervishes.

Although Islam had strict prohibitions against such type of ceremonies, there was great support of the arts under the Seljuk rule in Konya and a pronounced freedom which made it possible for the Sema ceremony to take place.

According to Turkish scholar Abdülbakî Gölpinarli, "Mevlânâ would easily be impressed by daily events and would start reciting his feelings while he was performing semâ in ecstasy and pour them into the mould [sic] of measure and rhyme."[7] Is it any wonder, then, that Rumi would make so many references to musical instruments in his poetry?

---

[7] Erol, *Mevlânâ's Life*, 32.

Poet-Musician Playing a Tanbur
Excavated ceramic from Anatolia, early 13th century.

Photo Credit: bpkBildagentur/Museum of Islamic Art/
Georg Niedermeiser/ Art Resource, NY.

Musical Instruments Commonly Referred to in Rumi's Poetry

Ney (or nay, from Persian nāy meaning reed, pipe.) The end-blown flute of the Middle East, from North Africa to Iran and the Caucasus. Made of cane (or sometimes wood or metal), it is often the only wind instrument regularly used in classical ensembles of Middle-Eastern music. Its characteristically breathy tone gives much scope for 'programme' effects, like the blowing of the wind or the shepherd's mourning. Famously, Rumi begins his *Mesnevî* with the couplet:

> "Listen to this Ney, while it's complaining,
> The story of separation from God it's explaining."[8]

Rebab (or rabab.) The oldest known Arabic word for a bowed instrument today denoting a large number of instruments played from North Africa across Asia to Indonesia. Pear- and boat-shaped rabābs hollowed in one piece, held downwards, and consisting of a membrane belly and two or three thick gut strings were particularly common. Flat, round, trapezoidal and rectangular bodies are also found. The single-stringed "poet's fiddle" of the Arab Middle East has a small round or cylindrical body that appears skewered by a narrow neck, and is played especially in self-accompaniment to narrations.

---
[8] Erol, *Mevlânâ's Life*, 31.

Tanbur A very early name for a long lute with a full metallic timbre, today denoting many varieties over the Middle East from Syria and Iraq to Turkestan in Central Asia. It has a small pear-shaped body, a long neck, many gut frets and two or three double metal strings. It has faithfully preserved the outer appearance of the ancient lutes of Babylonia and Egypt.

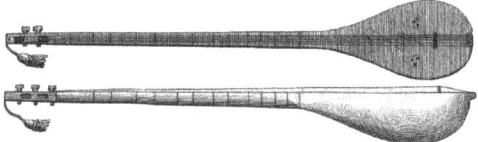

Saz The 'long lute of Turkey' played also to the east up to Azerbaijan on the Caspian and in Europe in local varieties across to Albania on the Adriatic and Greece. Similar to tanbur, it has a long thin neck, three double metal strings, and a pear-shaped body that has, from the side, a characteristic appearance of a deep scoop, deepest at the level of the bridge.

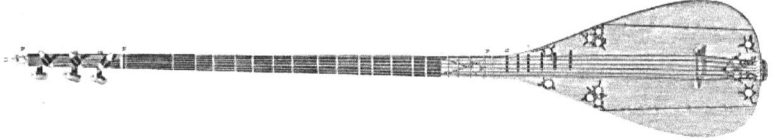

Tambourine A frame drum consisting of a single skin and pairs of metallic jingles placed within the frame. Essential to much classical music, it appears in the Middle Ages first in the Middle East and by c.1300 in Europe. Over the Middle East and North Africa, tambourines are played with subtle use of both hands in the membrane, the fingers of the holding hand participating, whereas common European manner involves striking and shaking.

Zurna (or surna, surnāy, from Persian sūr meaning feast, and nāy meaning reed, pipe.) The oriental representative of the shawm family, an end-blown oboe played to Central Eurasia, western Asia and North Africa. It consists of seven finger holes, one thumb hole, and several 'vent' holes. Historically played outdoors during festive events and to gather crowds in order to make official announcements, it produces a constantly loud, high-pitched and piercing sound.

The Story of Joseph and Jacob

Rumi mentions Joseph and Jacob in his rubáiyát more often than characters from any other story. Not only is the story of Joseph and his father Jacob given prominence in the Quran, but it is a dominant reference throughout Persian, Urdu and Arabic poetry as well, where Joseph is the symbol of the one who has left or been pulled away and Jacob is the symbol of the yearning lover.

The story of Joseph is shared in both the Bible (Genesis chapters 37, 38-50) and the Quran (which names its twelfth chapter, "Joseph"). There are slight differences in the two accounts. This summary is based on the story as it is presented in the Quran.

In his lifetime, Joseph went through intense suffering, but he was also given many spiritual blessings.

Of the family's twelve boys, Joseph was his father Jacob's favorite. Because of their jealousy, the brothers took Joseph into the wilderness and threw him into a well. They returned home, lying to their father, saying that his favorite son had been eaten by a wolf.

In the meantime, some strangers found Joseph, pulled him out of the well, and sold him as a slave to a prosperous Egyptian man and his family.

After some years of working for the Egyptians, Joseph was falsely accused of committing adultery with the Egyptian's wife. He was unjustly thrown into jail at the same time as two other men. Joseph successfully interpreted the dreams of these two other men. Eventually, one of the two was released and returned to his job of serving the King.

Several years passed. The King had two confusing dreams which no one could interpret. The former inmate remembered Joseph's talent, so he returned to the jail to ask Joseph for his help. Joseph saw the dreams as a prophecy for the entire region: there would be seven years of plenty, followed by seven years of famine. The inmate shared this interpretation with the King. The King was so pleased with the interpretation's clarity and vision that he summoned Joseph from jail and put him in charge of Egypt's granaries.

Joseph prepared Egypt for the famine by storing grain during the seven years of plenty. During the years of famine, Joseph's brothers, sent by their father, came to Egypt to purchase grain. They didn't recognize Joseph, although he recognized them. He sent them back home with grain, as well as his shirt.

Jacob had become blind with grief after the disappearance of his favorite son. As soon as his other sons arrived back home from Egypt, he caught the scent of Joseph's shirt. In this way, he came to know that Joseph was still alive. Then, when the sons covered his face with the shirt, Jacob regained his eyesight.

Finally, at Joseph's invitation, the entire tribe joined Joseph in Egypt to live happy and prosperous lives.

Both Joseph and Jacob are considered prophets.

The Concordance

With this publication, as Ergin intended with *Mevlânâ Rubâîler*, we are not trying to create controversy. Like so many others, we believe that these are sacred texts. And, we believe the more clear water poured into the river, the better. We encourage all who are interested to compare *The Ergin Translations* with the work of other translators.

You will notice in this Concordance that we have included a source for Ergin's original translations of Ergin's *Mevlânâ Rubâîler*, as well as for those of Turkish scholar Abdülbakî Gölpinarli, Persian scholar Badî'uzzamân Forûzânfar and Turkish scholar and spiritual leader Şefik Can. We have depended on Ergin's source numbers for these three. As Ergin states in the Translator's Note to his *Mevlânâ Rubâîler*, "For each of the quatrains, there are three sources cited. This is due to conflicting scholarship as regards original material."[9]

Also included in our Concordance are the rubai numbers corresponding to the work, *The Quatrains of Rumi*, by the Persian scholars Ibrahim Gamard and Rawan Farhadi. The Gamard-Farhadi book is well-researched, and we were able to ascertain from it any of the few Forûzânfar concordances which were missing from Ergin's work.

---

[9]Nevit Ergin and Merâle Ekmekçioğlu, *Mevlânâ Rubâîler* (Konya: Saray Medya Yayinlari, 2016), 13.

Rubáiyát	Duplicate numbers	Ergin	Gölpinarli	Forûzânfar	Şefik Can	Farhadi Gamard
\multicolumn{7}{c}{**VOLUME 4**}						
\multicolumn{7}{c}{*Dîvân-i Kebîr Replica, Volume 2, Page 166b*}						
1399		303-1	156-146	1362	1498	805
1400		292-2	156-147	1223	1360	403
1401		292-4	156-148	1109	1247	1238
1402		294-3	156-149	1323	1459	337
1403		294-4	156-150	1147	1285	222
1404		304-3	156-151	1119	1257	1896
1405		293-1	156-152	1107	1245	1237
1406		294-2	157-153	1224	1361	1379
1407		293-3	157-154	1352	1488	1086
1408		304-4	157-155	1151	1289	1134
1409		295-2	157-156	1157	1295	1384
1410		307-1	157-157	1170	1308	1353
1411		306-1	157-158	1178	1316	668
1412		305-1	157-159	1272	1409	541
1413		305-3	157-160	1175	1313	738
1414		306-3	158-161	1129	1267	986
1415		305-2	158-162	1227	1364	1026
1416		307-2	158-163	1361	1497	562
1417		308-3	158-164	1132	1270	802
1418		308-2	158-165	1172	1310	1005
1419		308-1	158-166	1364	1500	701
1420	625	307-4	139-2	1166	1304	1882
1421		310-2	158-167	1126	1264	697
\multicolumn{7}{c}{*Dîvân-i Kebîr Replica, Volume 2, Page 167a*}						
1422		414-1	189-75	1643	1828	621
1423		380-3	192-23	1523	1699	844
1424		380-4	192-24	1554	1730	997
1425		380-2	192-25	1536	1712	1603
1426		379-4	192-26	1572	1748	259
1427		379-2	192-27	1524	1700	902

Rubáiyát	Duplicate numbers	Ergin	Gölpinarli	Forûzânfar	Şefik Can	Farhadi Gamard
1428		379-3	193-28	1550	1726	593
1429		383-4	193-29	1563	1739	1395
1430		384-2	193-30	1575	1751	532
1431		382-2	193-31	1566	1742	518
1432		384-4	193-32	1585	1761	5
1433		382-1	193-33	1545	1721	73
1434		381-1	193-34	1561	1737	915
1435		381-3	193-35	1560	1735	478
1436		383-3	193-36	1556	1732	1188
1437		384-3	194-37	1553	1729	996
1438		384-1	194-38	1581	1757	753
1439		381-4	194-39	1580	1756	791
1440		385-1	194-40	1582	1758	1618
1441		385-2	194-41	1559	1735	1823
1442		385-4	194-42	1548	1724	946
1443		385-3	194-43	1522	1698	426
1444		387-4	194-44	1532	1708	1089
1445		387-3	194-45	1538	1714	1035
1446		386-3	195-46	1547	1723	209
1447		387-1	195-47	1541	1717	1131
1448		389-1	195-48	1537	1713	1036
1449		389-2	195-49	1535	1711	178
1450		389-4	195-50	1555	2731	298
1451		390-1	195-51	1525	1701	237
1452		390-3	195-52	1527	1703	490
1453		391-1	195-53	1568	1744	519
1454		392-1	196-54	1577	1753	607
Dîvân-i Kebîr Replica, Volume 2, Page 167b						
1455		391-2	196-55	1544	1720	1979
1456	1010	475-2	210-113	1848	2041	1155
1457		391-3	196-56	1570	1746	662
1458		392-2	196-57	1526	1702	1102

Rubáiyát	Duplicate numbers	Ergin	Gölpinarli	Forûzânfar	Şefik Can	Farhadi Gamard
1459		392-4	196-58	1567	1743	520
1460	1028	393-1	196-59	1898	1763	1607
1461		392-3	196-60	1551	1727	654
1462		393-2	196-61	1530	1706	166
1463		393-3	197-62	1546	1722	1513
1464		393-4	197-63	1578	1754	1560
1465		394-2	197-64	1569	1745	1956
1466		394-1	197-65	1571	1747	457
1467		417-4	219-187	1805	1998	1111
1468		419-3	219-188	1681	1875	1731
1469		418-4	220-189	1893	2085	525
1470	898	420-1	197-1	1804	1997	151
1471		421-1	220-190	1857	2050	1817
1472		421-2	220-191	1737	1930	333
1473		421-3	220-192	1983	2175	203
1474		422-3	220-193	1906	2098	502
1475		422-2	220-194	1940	2132	521
1476		421-4	220-195	1717	1910	1106
1477		414-2	220-196	1960	2152	645
1478		415-4	221-197	1859	2052	190
1479		415-3	221-198	1949	2141	1758
1480		416-4	221-199	1943	2135	606
1481		415-2	221-200	1972	2164	954
1482	1822	423-1	221-201	1813	2006/ 2178	982
1483		414-4	221-202	1809	2002	1672
1484		415-1	221-203	1837	2030	781
1485		427-3	221-204	1013	2127	824
1486		416-1	221-205	1691	1885	1562
1487		414-3	222-206	1867	2060	451
Dîvân-i Kebîr Replica, Volume 2, Page 168a						
1488		146-3	103-310	751	804	1257
1489		146-4	103-311	562	617	1290

Rubáiyát	Duplicate numbers	Ergin	Gölpinarli	Forûzânfar	Şefik Can	Farhadi Gamard
1490		150-3	103-312	744	797	1621
1491		161-3	103-313	770	823	1390
1492		163-3	103-314	447	502	1638
1493		167-1	103-315	846	898	932
1494		164-1	104-316	624	678	1154
1495	1095	164-4	104-317	772	825	1413
1496		165-1	104-318	844	896	367
1497		166-4	104-319	837	889	1306
1498		163-1	104-320	863	915	1391
1499		168-4	104-321	604	---	1405
1500	300	167-2	76-77	785	837	1716
1501		168-2	104-322	475	530	1354
1502		162-4	104-323	553	608	1966
1503		169-4	104-324	832	884	1674
1504		169-3	105-325	478	533	1269
1505		169-1	105-326	460	515	620
1506	1804	168-1	101-297	474	529	356
1507		171-4	105-327	825	877	609
1508		171-2	105-328	565	620	1683
1509		170-1	105-329	775	827	633
1510	1771	172-3	97-266	573	628	571
1511		173-1	105-330	445	500	383
1512		174-4	105-331	792	844	1678
1513		174-3	105-332	601	---	1778
1514		173-3	---	781	833	95
1515		178-2	105-333	840	892	315
1516		176-4	106-334	779	831	1499
1517		176-3	106-335	798	850	220
1518		177-3	106-336	826	878	1447
1519	1273	178-1	106-337	799	851	218
1520		171-1	81-123	628	682	1297

Dîvân-i Kebîr Replica, Volume 2, Page 168b

1521		181-3	106-338	602	656	1509

Rubáiyát	Duplicate numbers	Ergin	Gölpinarli	Forûzânfar	Şefik Can	Farhadi Gamard
1522		181-4	106-339	871	923	745
1523		181-1	106-340	603	657	1967
1524		182-4	106-341	632	686	1194
1525		182-1	106-342	853	905	1577
1526		184-1	107-343	501	556	394
1527		182-3	107-344	504	559	693
1528		183-3	107-345	711	765	567
1529		186-2	107-346	634	688	1231
1530		188-1	107-347	471	526	631
1531		187-3	107-348	841	893	679
1532		187-1	107-349	789	841	558
1533		189-1	107-350	530	585	866
1534		189-2	108-351	758	811	491
1535		189-3	108-352	647	701	544
1536		190-2	108-353	568	623	1103
1537		192-3	108-354	815	---	588
1538		192-2	108-355	446	501	1965
1539		190-1	108-356	444	499	379
1540		191-4	108-357	491	546	406
1541		193-1	108-358	539	594	1400
1542		192-4	109-359	801	853	670
1543		199-4	109-360	479	938	213
1544		194-3	109-361	459	514	1138
1545		199-2	109-362	843	---	1372
1546		200-3	109-363	---	955	---
1547		197-3	109-364	705	759	1440
1548		196-3	109-366	828	880	1118
1549		196-2	110-367	455	510	1576
1550		198-4	110-368	542	597	1585
1551	315	194-4	110-369	435	---	117
1552		201-1	110-370	578	633	1857
1553		203-2	110-371	786	838	359

Rubáiyát	Duplicate numbers	Ergin	Gölpinarli	Forûzânfar	Şefik Can	Farhadi Gamard
Dîvân-i Kebîr Replica, Volume 2, Page 169a						
1554		358-2	176-76	1474	1637	473
1555		359-4	176-77	1497	1660	239
1556		360-4	176-78	1423	1586	611
1557		361-3	176-79	1435	1598	158
1558		360-2	176-80	1494	1657	1126
1559		362-1	176-81	1450	1613	1671
1560		373-2	---	---	---	---
1561		362-4	177-82	1415	1578	225
1562		459-3	177-83	1902	---	1983
1563	1576	361-4	177-84	1428	1591	1954
1564		364-3	177-85	1496	1659	1143
1565		364-4	177-86	1430	1593	345
1566		365-2	177-87	1469	1632	286
1567		363-3	177-88	1506	1669	234
1568		366-4	177-89	1373	1536	152
1569		367-3	177-90	1376	1539	1230
1570		367-2	178-91	1508	1671	789
1571		368-4	178-92	1505	1668	137
1572		370-2	178-93	1461	1624	1760
1573		370-4	178-94	1493	1656	251
1574		370-3	178-95	1375	1538	1764
1575		371-2	178-96	1426	1589	612
1576	1563	372-1	178-97	1428	1686	1954
1577		372-4	179-98	1519	1682	1459
1578		372-2	179-99	1465	1628	1214
1579		373-3	179-100	1500	1663	1206
1580		373-4	179-101	1507	1670	1838
1581		375-2	179-102	1394	1557	963
1582		376-2	179-103	1438	1601	813
1583		376-4	179-104	1421	1584	750
1584		377-3	179-105	1378	1541	671

Rubáiyát	Duplicate numbers	Ergin	Gölpinarli	Forûzânfar	Şefik Can	Farhadi Gamard
1585		378-1	180-106	1369	1532	1709
1586		378-2	180-107	1477	1640	353
Dîvân-i Kebîr Replica, Volume 2, Page 169b						
1587		378-4	180-108	1511	1674	1186
1588		378-3	180-109	1520	1683	537
1589		395-3	185-45	1596	1781	1805
1590		395-4	---	1639	1824	1258
1591		403-2	185-46	1654	1836	82
1592		402-2	186-47	1592	1777	957
1593		401-1	186-48	1653	1837	346
1594		402-1	186-49	1659	1838	61
1595		397-2	186-50	1970	1839	535
1596		399-3	186-51	1647	1840	293
1597		400-4	186-52	1605	1790	1866
1598		398-1	186-53	1602	1787	528
1599		399-2	186-54	1649	1841	507
1600		397-3	187-55	1615	1800	948
1601		397-4	187-56	1613	1798	980
1602		403-3	187-57	1617	1802	231
1603		404-2	187-58	1635	1820	1613
1604		405-3	187-59	1657	1843	60
1605		405-4	187-60	1595	1780	1355
1606		407-4	187-61	1634	1819	703
1607		406-4	187-62	1969	1845	1650
1608		367-1	188-63	1638	1823	595
1609		408-4	188-64	1623	1808	1757
1610		409-2	188-65	1604	1789	26
1611		409-4	188-66	1663	1847	1212
1612		410-1	188-67	1616	1801	323
1613		410-2	188-68	1636	1821	647
1614		410-3	188-69	1637	1822	327
1615		411-3	188-70	1619	1804	1324
1616		411-4	189-71	1621	1806	1676

Rubáiyát	Duplicate numbers	Ergin	Gölpinarli	Forûzânfar	Şefik Can	Farhadi Gamard
1617		412-1	189-72	1590	1775	206
1618		412-2	189-73	1597	1782	390
1619		413-2	189-74	1622	1807	1675
Dîvân-i Kebîr Replica, Volume 2, Page 170a						
1620		202-2	110-372	709	763	565
1621		202-1	110-373	712	766	566
1622		323-1	158-168	1154	1292	415
1623		204-2	110-374	861	913	1512
1624		205-3	111-375	571	626	1226
1625		205-2	111-376	563	618	154
1626	318	202-3	111-377	480	535	887
1627		207-3	111-378	716	770	1589
1628		209-2	111-379	552	607	174
1629		209-4	111-380	576	631	663
1630		211-4	111-381	657	711	706
1631	457	211-1	111-382	585	---	1441
1632		213-3	112-383	855	907	141
1633		212-4	112-384	833	885	438
1634		212-3	112-385	510	565	385
1635		214-1	112-386	599	653	1279
1636		214-4	112-387	609	663	891
1637		215-2	112-388	637	691	391
1638		215-4	112-389	635	689	1244
1639		217-2	112-390	541	596	788
1640		218-2	113-391	449	504	1469
1641		219-1	113-392	860	912	1542
1642		221-2	113-393	514	569	18
1643		221-3	113-394	470	525	1271
1644		222-2	113-395	442	497	1110
1645		223-2	113-396	638	692	1968
1646		223-4	113-397	797	849	1525
1647		224-2	113-398	457	512	691
1648		225-2	114-399	509	564	1302

Rubáiyát	Duplicate numbers	Ergin	Gölpinarli	Forûzânfar	Şefik Can	Farhadi Gamard
1649		224-4	114-400	490	545	236
1650		227-1	114-401	865	917	1974
1651		226-2	114-402	820	872	1031
1652		227-2	114-403	777	829	526
Dîvân-i Kebîr Replica, Volume 2, Page 170b						
1653		226-4	114-404	586	641	534
1654		225-1	114-405	695	749	1711
1655		228-2	114-406	522	577	1503
1656		228-4	115-407	851	903	328
1657		229-2	115-408	---	925	---
1658		229-1	115-409	---	969	---
1659		229-3	115-410	582	637	1144
1660		230-3	115-411	755	808	1247
1661		230-1	115-412	831	883	1702
1662		230-2	115-413	807	859	267
1663		232-4	115-414	626	680	1000
1664		234-3	116-415	784	836	1457
1665		236-1	116-416	806	858	183
1666		236-2	116-417	752	805	1551
1667		238-1	116-418	495	550	1365
1668		238-4	116-419	765	818	726
1669		239-4	116-420	850	902	435
1670		241-3	116-421	701	755	1510
1671		241-4	116-422	794	---	910
1672	475	244-2	96-251	769	822	1581
1673		243-1	116-423	868	920	242
1674		247-1	117-424	814	866	885
1675		247-2	117-425	481	536	1490
1676		243-2	117-426	482	537	665
1677		246-2	117-427	762	815	488
1678		246-3	117-428	486	541	905
1679		245-1	117-429	700	754	793

Rubáiyát	Duplicate numbers	Ergin	Gölpinarli	Forûzânfar	Şefik Can	Farhadi Gamard
1680		242-4	117-430	597	651	1612
1681		245-2	117-431	472	527	1284
1682		245-4	117-432	750	803	1665
1683		243-4	118-433	793	845	1293
1684		248-1	118-434	561	616	1643
1685		247-4	118-435	817	869	41
		Dîvân-i Kebîr Replica, Volume 2, Page 171a				
1686		309-3	159-169	1211	1348	1007
1687		309-2	159-170	1281	1418	318
1688		312-2	159-171	1140	1278	419
1689		312-1	159-172	1360	1496	1453
1690		310-4	159-173	1278	1415	1122
1691		311-1	159-174	1201	1339	1063
1692		314-4	159-175	1161	1299	408
1693		316-3	159-176	1341	1477	1386
1694		312-3	160-177	1113	1251	1330
1695		315-2	160-178	1125	1263	1020
1696		314-1	160-179	1117	1255	715
1697		315-3	160-180	1264	1401	1133
1698		314-2	160-181	1158	1296	868
1699		313-4	160-182	1148	1286	139
1700		313-2	160-183	1271	1408	1066
1701		312-4	160-184	1292	1429	734
1702		317-1	161-185	1354	1490	97
1703		317-4	161-186	1261	1398	889
1704		318-3	161-187	1198	1336	899
1705		318-4	161-188	1324	1460	1448
1706		319-1	161-189	1143	1281	341
1707		319-3	161-190	1327	1463	1340
1708		319-2	161-191	1208	1345	1117
1709		319-4	161-192	1343	1479	1300
1710		321-1	161-193	1217	1354	1164
1711		320-1	162-194	1250	---	1092

Rubáiyát	Duplicate numbers	Ergin	Gölpinarli	Forûzânfar	Şefik Can	Farhadi Gamard
1712		320-3	162-195	1120	1258	388
1713		321-4	162-196	1295	1432	1601
1714		320-4	162-197	1219	1356	474
1715		322-3	162-198	1284	1421	109
1716		324-4	162-199	1301	1438	1359
1717		325-4	162-200	1353	1489	1139
1718		327-1	156-148	1108	1246	1236
Dîvân-i Kebîr Replica, Volume 2, Page 171b						
1719		327-3	162-201	1168	1306	906
1720		327-4	163-202	1162	1300	1381
1721		328-2	163-203	1165	1303	777
1722		328-3	163-204	1244	1381	424
1723		329-1	163-205	1138	1276	857
1724		329-3	163-206	1310	1447	811
1725		329-4	163-207	1233	1370	1506
1726		330-3	163-208	1182	1320	1255
1727		330-4	163-209	1334	1470	1481
1728		331-4	164-210	1216	1353	1934
1729		332-1	164-211	1240	1377	1150
1730		332-2	164-212	1344	1480	1521
1731		333-3	164-213	1215	1352	280
1732		335-2	164-214	1273	1410	1072
1733		336-4	164-215	1318	1454	666
1734		337-4	164-216	1339	1475	343
1735		335-3	164-217	1207	1344	476
1736		337-1	165-218	1267	1404	669
1737		336-3	165-219	1290	1427	185
1738		338-4	165-220	1190	1328	845
1739		338-1	165-221	1181	1319	642
1740		340-2	165-222	1133	1271	503
1741		343-1	165-223	1262	1399	629
1742		341-4	165-224	1306	1443	863
1743		342-4	165-225	1291	1428	1382

Rubáiyát	Duplicate numbers	Ergin	Gölpinarli	Forûzânfar	Şefik Can	Farhadi Gamard
1744		344-2	166-226	1316	1453	854
1745		342-3	166-227	1314	1451	1892
1746		341-1	166-228	1363	1499	827
1747		344-3	166-229	1141	1279	311
1748		344-4	166-230	1326	1462	1341
1749		345-1	166-231	1268	1405	1210
1750		345-3	166-232	1160	1298	849
1751		346-2	166-233	1193	1331	396

Dîvân-i Kebîr Replica, Volume 2, Page 172a

Rubáiyát	Duplicate numbers	Ergin	Gölpinarli	Forûzânfar	Şefik Can	Farhadi Gamard
1752		134-4	65-314	265	283	303
1753		135-1	65-315	344	362	766
1754		134-1	65-316	286	304	1483
1755		132-4	66-317	224	242	651
1756		133-4	66-318	139	157	1485
1757		133-2	66-319	223	241	153
1758		135-2	66-320	332	350	1084
1759		132-3	66-321	240	258	938
1760	1315/1343	136-4	61-276	407	425	643
1761		136-2	66-322	305	323	350
1762		137-1	66-323	357	375	85
1763		137-2	66-324	353	371	884
1764		138-2	67-4	433	488	911
1765		150-4	97-261	454	509	103
1766	245/1798	153-4	70-22	852	904	1047
1767		152-4	97-262	720	774	470
1768		160-1	97-263	733	786	1273
1769		159-4	97-264	524	579	787
1770		161-4	97-265	641	695	763
1771	1510	172-4	97-266	573	628	571
1772		178-3	97-267	682	736	1289
1773	291	181-2	75-68	783	835	1814

Rubáiyát	Duplicate numbers	Ergin	Gölpinarli	Forûzânfar	Şefik Can	Farhadi Gamard
1774	366	183-2	83-143	537	592	1199
1775		183-4	98-269	512	567	1875
1776		184-4	98-270	651	705	1586
1777		187-2	98-271	692	746	1241
1778		191-3	98-272	515	570	655
1779		194-2	98-273	665	719	599
1780		196-1	98-274	671	725	118
1781		197-4	98-275	527	582	988
1782		194-1	99-276	723	777	1691
1783		203-4	99-277	747	800	1436
1784		203-3	99-278	669	723	760
Dîvân-i Kebîr Replica, Volume 2, Page 172b						
1785		204-4	99-279	529	584	463
1786		209-1	99-280	740	793	1431
1787		210-4	99-281	722	776	1270
1788		222-4	99-282	748	801	1417
1789		235-2	99-283	721	775	584
1790		235-4	100-284	679	733	1268
1791		236-3	100-285	525	580	1772
1792		248-3	100-286	519	574	1316
1793		248-2	100-287	518	573	1317
1794		246-4	100-288	862	914	320
1795		138-3	100-289	558	613	1173
1796		151-2	100-290	782	834	94
1797		153-2	100-291	778	830	505
1798	245/1766	154-2	70-22	852	904	1047
1799		156-4	101-292	572	627	895
1800	305	155-1	101-293	622	676	1812
1801		156-2	101-294	587	---	794
1802		152-2	101-295	656	710	1097
1803		159-2	101-296	476	531	387

Rubáiyát	Duplicate numbers	Ergin	Gölpinarli	Forûzânfar	Şefik Can	Farhadi Gamard
1804	1506	159-3	101-297	474	529	356
1805		160-2	101-298	760	813	1971
1806		161-1	101-299	606	660	249
1807		144-4	102-300	640	694	847
1808		142-1	102-301	564	619	1532
1809		142-3	102-302	450	505	1098
1810		144-2	102-303	456	511	1309
1811	239	141-3	69-16	659	713	1636
1812		144-3	102-304	856	908	1356
1813		147-3	102-305	854	906	851
1814		140-3	102-306	698	752	1152
1815		147-2	102-307	570	625	1088
1816		150-2	103-308	620	674	182
1817		145-4	103-309	802	854	582

Dîvân-i Kebîr Replica, Volume 2, Page 173a

Rubáiyát	Duplicate numbers	Ergin	Gölpinarli	Forûzânfar	Şefik Can	Farhadi Gamard
1818	1068	457-2	222-207	1963	2155	735
1819		454-4	222-208	1738	1931	1642
1820		457-4	222-209	1911	2103	1322
1821	1069	460-4	222-210	1946	2138	1380
1822	1482	463-3	222-211	1813	2006	982
1823	978	461-2	207-81	1754	1947	248
1824		462-4	222-212	1862	2055	1686
1825		463-1	222-213	1826	2019	47
1826		462-3	223-214	1811	2004	998
1827		467-3	223-215	1827	2020	953
1828		468-1	223-216	1698	1892	702
1829		468-2	223-217	1688	1882	384
1830		469-2	223-218	1858	2051	816
1831		470-4	223-219	1744	1937	281
1832		471-4	223-220	1801	1994	444
1833		471-3	223-221	1767	1960	1981
1834		476-4	224-222	1854	2047	1253
1835		477-1	224-223	1702	1896	1505

Rubáiyát	Duplicate numbers	Ergin	Gölpinarli	Forûzânfar	Şefik Can	Farhadi Gamard
1836		477-2	224-224	1699	1893	1184
1837		472-4	211-117	1736	1929	1553
1838		476-2	224-225	1739	1932	90
1839		473-3	224-226	1864	2057	1734
1840		472-1	224-227	1807	2000	271
1841		475-4	224-228	1732	1925	1550
1842		473-1	224-229	1891	2083	309
1843		477-3	224-230	1925	2117	1788
1844		474-1	225-231	1752	1945	1720
1845		472-2	225-232	1670	1864	968
1846	1071	480-3	218-173	1977	2169	416
1847	1072	478-2	218-174	1959	2151	1172
1848		479-2	225-233	1973	2165	322
1849		479-4	225-234	1677	1871	362
1850		482-2	225-235	1868	2061	1828
Dîvân-i Kebîr Replica, Volume 2, Page 173b						
1851		482-3	225-236	1695	1889	194
1852		482-4	225-237	1903	2095	903
1853		483-2	225-238	1936	2128	828
1854	1080	484-2	226-239	1766	1959	275
1855		484-3	226-240	1838	2031	560
1856		485-1	226-241	1742	1935	570
1857	1081	487-1	219-183	1855	2048	1337
1858	1074	488-3	218-176	1948	2140	1948
1859		488-1	226-242	1965	2157	335
1860		489-1	226-243	1711	---	1980
1861		490-1	226-244	1905	2097	1137
1862	1075	491-3	218-177	1954	2146	1107
1863		492-4	226-245	1885	2077	1727
1864		493-3	226-246	1879	2072	1093
1865		493-1	227-247	1890	2082	56
1866		494-2	227-248	1674	1868	1696
1867		495-1	227-249	1666	1860	173

Bibliography: *Mevlânâ Rubâîler*

Can, Şefik. *Hz. Mevlânâ'nin Rubâîleri*. Ankara, Turkey: T.C. Kûltûr Bakanliği Yayinlari/2752 Yayimlar Dairesi Başkanliği Sanat-Ebediyat Esereleri Dizise/3655-120, 2001.

Forüzânfar, Badî'uzzamân, ed. *Kulliyât-é shams yâdiwân-é kabîr-e mawlânâ jalâluddîn Muhammad mashhûrba-mawlawî*. Tehrân: University of Tehrân, 1957-1967.

Gölpinarli, Abdülbakî. *Dîvân-i Kebîr Mevlânâ Celâleddîn*. *I-VII*. Ankara: Turkey: Kûltûr Bakanliği, 1992.

_____. *Mevlânâ Celâleddîn, Rubâîler*. Ankara: Turkey: Ajans-Tûrk Matbaacilik Sanayi, 1982.

Bibliography: *The Rubáiyát of Rumi, The Ergin Translations*

Ergin, Nevit Oguz & Eçkmekçioğlu, Merâl. *Mevlânâ Rubâîler.* Konya: Sarayonu Gazete-Matbaa, 2016.

———. *Private Notes,* 2015.

Erol, Erdogan. *Mevlânâ's Life, Works and the Mevlânâ Museum.* Konya: Altunari Ofset Ltd. Şti, 2005.

Gamard, Ibrahim & Farhadi, Rawan. *The Quatrains of Rumi.* San Rafael, CA: Sufi Dari Books, 2008.

Rumi, Mevlânâ Celâleddîn. *Dîvân-i Kebîr, Meter 1*, Nevit O. Ergin, Translator. Walla Walla, WA: Turkish Ministry of Culture and Current, 1995.

———. *Dîvân-i Kebîr, Meter 10.* Nevit O. Ergin, Translator. Los Angeles, CA: Turkish Ministry of Culture and Echo Publications, 2000.

———. *Dîvân-i Kebîr Replica.* Compiled by Hasan ibni Osman-al Mavlavi, (1367-68). Konya: Altunari Ofset Ltd. Şti., 2007.

Shushud, Hasan. *Masters of Wisdom of Central Asia.* North Yorkshire, England: Coombe Springs Press, 1983.

Nevit O. Ergin
(1928-2015)

Nevit Ergin was a plastic surgeon. Although he continued to take frequent trips to his home country, Turkey, he lived the majority of his life in the United States, first in Michigan and then in Southern and finally Northern California. He is survived by five children and three grandchildren.

Dr. Ergin devoted himself to the same spiritual path as Rumi. The last 25 years of his life were used to bring more of Rumi's poetry and more awareness of Rumi's message to the Western world. Ergin's English translations are from the Turkish translations of Turkish scholar Abdülbakî Gölpinarli, and they are inspired. He was able to capture the essence of every verse he translated... and he translated over 44,000 verses.

As he liked to say, Ergin spent 60 years of his life "trying to get rid of this earth before it gets rid of me."

Other Works by Nevit O. Ergin

Crazy As We Are

The Dîvân-i Kebîr of Mevlânâ Celâleddîn Rumi
(Translation in 22 Volumes)

Divine Wine

Forbidden Rumi (with Will Johnson)

The Glory of Absence

Insane with Love (with Will Johnson)

Magnificent One

A Rose Garden

Mevlânâ Rubâîler (with Merâl Eçkmekçioğlu)

The Sufi Path of Annihilation

Tales of a Modern Sufi

Unknown Rumi

For those who would be interested in knowing Ergin's views on Rumi's quatrains, *Unknown Rumi* is a selection of 100 of the quatrains, with comments by Ergin on each of them.

Millicent Alexander
(1947-)

Millicent Alexander was born and raised in Los Angeles, California. She met Nevit Ergin at the home of Hasan Shushud in Istanbul, Turkey, in 1972. An account of her first meeting with these two remarkable men is included in *The Sufi Path of Annihilation* by Nevit O. Ergin (Inner Traditions).

That meeting was also her introduction to Itlak Yolu, the Sufi Path of Annihilation and Absolute Liberation, which embraces the universality of Rumi's messages. She has stayed on that path ever since.

She also stayed life-long friends with Nevit Ergin, working with him on bringing Rumi's poetry to the English-speaking world from 1992 (with the publication of *Crazy As We Are* [Holm Press]) until his passing in 2015.

Ms. Alexander is a retired educator and currently lives in Los Angeles, California.

Shahzad Mazhar
(1970-)

Shahzad Mazhar was born in Lahore, Pakistan. For his schooling, he was sent to St. Mary's Academy and finished his high school at Forman Christian College, Lahore. He was first exposed to Urdu and Persian poetry by his father, who was an officer in the Pakistani army. After high school, he traveled to the U.S.A. to study engineering. He was a partner in a computer manufacturing company in his twenties and thirties.

His interest in Rumi since his early twenties exposed him to the translations of Dr. Nevit Ergin. Further inquiry brought him into contact with Millicent Alexander, who provided him with the opportunity to be part of a team bringing Ergin's translations to the world, translations of the extraordinary poetry of the spiritual Master known in the West as Rumi.

A Final Note

Love could be metaphorical or real. Metaphorical love is an attraction between individuals or from a person to God. Real, pure Love manifests and overwhelms the wayfarer. [. . .] Its source is not from outside, but intrinsic. In this Love, Lover and Beloved are the same. It is intoxication, inebriation and the fruit of Annihilation.

-Hasan Lutfi Shushud
Masters of Wisdom, 127.

www.ingramcontent.com/pod-product-compliance
Lightning Source LLC
LaVergne TN
LVHW070040120526
838202LV00110B/2648/J